DEATH, MONEY AND THE VULTURES

DEATH, MONEY AND THE VULTURES

Inheritance and avarice, 1660–1750

John Addy

London and New York

First published 1992
by Routledge
11 New Fetter Lane, London EC4P 4EE

Simultaneously published in the USA and Canada
by Routledge
a division of Routledge, Chapman and Hall, Inc.
29 West 35th Street, New York, NY 10001

Typeset in 10 on 12 point Palatino by
Falcon Typographic Ltd, Fife, Scotland
Printed in Great Britain by
TJ Press (Padstow) Ltd, Padstow, Cornwall

British Library Cataloguing in Publication Data
Addy, John
Death, money and the vultures.
I. Title
344.20654

Library of Congress Cataloging in Publication Data

Addy, John
Death, money, and the vultures / John Addy.
p.   cm.
Includes bibliographical references and index.
1. Wills–Great Britain–History.   2. Decedents' estates–Great
Britain–History.   3. Great Britain–Social life and customs.
I.   Title.
KD1509.A33   1992
346.4105'4–dc20
[344.10654]   92–13974

ISBN 0–415–05031–6

I appreciate the generous support given
to me by Professor G. P. McGregor

CONTENTS

CONTENTS

PREFACE

My experience acting as a guest lecturer to Family History Societies and those engaged in population studies encouraged me to search for additional sources of information. Working in the consistory court files enabled me to discover this additional source, which provided an insight into what often lay behind the wills and inventories of the deceased.

The allegations brought by one party against another, together with the depositions of the witnesses, enable a fairly accurate assessment of the relationship, attitudes and morality of those who became engaged in contesting wills.

This study is the product of many years of work in sorting consistory court files, which reveal material that could be used to look at society in closely related areas. This book is the result of investigating the disputes not of the great but rather of those in humbler circumstances such as weavers, farmers, yeomen, masons, wheelwrights, blacksmiths and small merchants – the ones who do not figure in the general history books but who do contribute towards the making of history.

This has not been an easy study to compile, for secondary material on contested wills is virtually non-existent. There is also the factor that many of the files were so fragile that it was impossible to use them, or so fragmentary that to build up a case was difficult. If this study widens the field of research then I shall feel amply rewarded for my efforts.

John Addy
University College of Ripon and York St John
York

ACKNOWLEDGMENTS

I owe a debt of gratitude to the following who have assisted me during the preparation of this study: Dr David Smith of the Borthwick Institute of Historical Research, York, Mr Ian Dunn of the Cheshire Record Office, Chester, Mr K. Hall of the Lancashire Record Office, Preston, Mr W. Connor of the Leeds District Archives, the Bishop of Gloucester for permission to use the Consistory Court records, Dr J. A. Sharpe of the University of York for permission to quote from *Early Modern England* (chapter 8), to Peter Earle for permission to quote the letter on p. 304 in his *Making of the English Middle Class*; also to Mr G. C. F. Forster of the University of Leeds for his advice and Professor G. P. McGregor, who has provided me with facilities at the University College of Ripon and York St John to complete this study; finally to Mrs Diana Wetherall–Terry who has read the script and suggested certain improvements.

ABBREVIATIONS

BIHR	Borthwick Institute of Historical Research
CRO	Cheshire Record Office
GDRO	Gloucester Diocesan Record Office
LDA	Leeds District Archives
LRO	Lancashire Record Office

1

INTRODUCTION

'Where there's a will, there's a relative.'

This very basic comment has been known in the north, and in all probability in other parts of the country, for centuries to indicate what was, in all likelihood, the origin of a contested will.

Any investigation into the study of wills, which were the subject of a cause in the consistory courts, promoted by disappointed relatives, intimate friends or creditors of the deceased, is no light task. It is clear from the number of enquiries made and searches undertaken into this interesting subject that little, if anything, has been produced. Although contested wills are now listed in several county and diocesan record offices, their study has not so far proved to be of sufficient interest to students and others who are looking for a suitable subject for research. Probably this reluctance arises from the problems that face those who undertake such a study when confronted by the legal processes of the consistory court.

It is important that the origin of the will and the difference between a will and a testament should be understood. In the matter of probate and administration of the estate of a deceased person, the custom until 1692 was very different in the northern province from that prevailing in the southern one. The church became involved in proving wills at an early date, so it is in the diocesan archives that evidence on this subject is to be found until the whole business was taken over by the state in 1857.

An important central point in this study is the attitude towards death as disclosed in diaries, letters and funeral accounts, for these reveal the opinions held by relatives and neighbours towards the deceased and sometimes vice versa. The church

1

was concerned to ensure that parishioners died not just at peace with their neighbours but 'in love and charity with all men', as the Prayer Book phrases it. Therefore the church considered it a duty to encourage all men and women to make a will and the clergy were to assist parishioners in drawing up their wills.[1] The clergy also had a secular interest in death because they were able to collect mortuary dues from all those parishioners who died while in the parish. Although the Mortuaries Act of 1534/5 had imposed limitations on the levying of such dues, they continued to be collected in the diocese of Chester, basically on the grounds that parts of the north were areas of serious poverty and the clergy needed such fees to augment their pitifully low stipends; these dues were not finally abolished until 1763.[2]

The preamble to a will usually, but not always, includes some reference to the religious beliefs of the deceased, coupled with instructions as to the disposal of his earthly remains. Families which had obtained a faculty for a burial place within the church, be it in the chancel or the nave, considered that this gave them a right to erect a family pew above the burial vault. These rights families jealously protected, often disputing their title with others who claimed to have a similar concession. Such pews were classified as private property; therefore they could be bequeathed in a will or sold, or the title to their occupation could be disputed between members of the family, generally relatives. Not only the possession of a private pew but also ownership of land, manufactured and other goods (such as the contents of a wine merchant's cellar in Halifax or a clothier's equipment in Bradford) could all provide grounds for a legal contest which in the end could be very costly.[3]

The vultures are many and varied, ranging from close and distant relatives to intimate friends claiming that the deceased had promised to remember them in his will. One allegation that is often found is that the will had been drawn up after the testator had died. Another allegation is that the deceased's goods and chattels were grossly undervalued in the inventory or sold at ridiculously low prices. Then there were the executors who failed to pay legacies or creditors who moved in to remove goods as payment for debt, or the negligent guardians of minors, all of whom served to bring business to the consistory court.

The classifying and listing of contested wills in detail has uncovered a considerable number that were more or less fiercely contested. A preliminary study of such wills in the northern province and the diocese of Gloucester has revealed an area of study, largely unexplored, which throws light on a society where all the seven deadly sins are to be found alive and flourishing. Closely connected with this subject are the attitudes towards disease and death, the former dreaded because a serious illness usually terminated in death, the latter (and its companion, burial) playing a part in the lives of our seventeenth- and eighteenth-century ancestors that was considered very important and called for great solemnity.

Part I

SUMMONING
THE VULTURES

2

LAST WILLS AND TESTAMENTS

Before moving to a detailed study of contested wills and the kind of society in which legal disputes took place, it is advisable to have an understanding of what last wills really are. The key documents involved in any study of this nature are those known as the 'last will and testament', to which is often attached an inventory of the deceased person's goods and chattels, both movable and immovable. It is these that, in one way or another, form the basis of many disputes. Although numerous studies of wills and probate inventories have been undertaken for several areas of the country, they do not appear to have been followed up in depth.

The history of the will, especially its origin, is obscure. In England the structure of the will indicates a Scandinavian rather than a Roman origin. Therefore, the tradition of making a will is much stronger in the north than in the south. One point is quite clear: succession, resulting from law and custom, precedes the legal power to dispose of one's real property by will; this is known as Realty.

The second document, the testament, dealt with personal property or effects and was known as Personalty. At some date, not now possible to determine, the two were combined in a single document in the same manner as they are found at the present time. It is important to remember that real property is always devised, but personal property is bequeathed.

According to Henry Massie in his study of *Ancient Law*,[1] the custom of making a will spread throughout Europe purely from the influence of the church. The clergy were familiar with canon law but in the twelfth century the revival of Roman law, with its centralized style, influenced the interpretation of canon law, making it far more rigid. The church has always benefited from its involvement in probate because it received income from the fees that were charged for proving or authenticating wills. A study of the English will has been accurately recorded by Pollock and Maitland in their *History of English Law*:

> Nothing is plainer than that the so called Anglo-Saxon will is not the Roman testament, for the Anglo-Saxon will . . . seems to have grown upon English soil, and the Roman testament had little to do with its development.[2]

Medieval common law, while strictly retaining its jurisdiction over land or real property, for some undeclared reason left control over personal property chiefly to the church. Therefore in England the task of proving wills and supervising the distribution of a deceased person's property, with certain exceptions, came under the jurisdiction of the consistory courts;[3] this also included the estates of those persons who died intestate until the whole business was transferred to the state in 1857.

Matters were further complicated by the difference between the northern and southern provinces in the law concerning wills; a difference that was only resolved, in the supervision of the disposal of personal property, in 1692. This difference was known as the 'custom of York'. This custom, if it did not originate with the state, crew up under its auspices. Quite early a conflict arose between the claims of the lord of the manor, the deceased man's wife and children and the church concerning the disposal of the deceased person's goods and chattels. Hence it was considered reasonable to divide the goods into three parts of equal value, one to the lord, one to the deceased's wife and children and one to the church. Very quickly the lord's claim was converted into the medieval *heriot*, which later became a mortuary due, thus leaving two-thirds to the wife and children, which became known as the *pars rationalibus* or 'wife's part' and 'child's part'. All that the church did was to use the third part to pay the debts and funeral expenses of the deceased, and to pay for requiem masses to be said for the repose of the deceased person's soul, and to organize the distribution of the remainder to charity in accordance with the wishes of the deceased.[4] Towards the close of the thirteenth century, as the feudal system began to decay so the methods concerning the disposal of land changed. Feudal custom was replaced by the emergence of life estates based on the right of primogeniture.

As wills gradually became part of the fabric of society, someone had to be responsible for drawing up a will at a time when the majority of people were illiterate or at best semi-literate. This duty fell on the shoulders of the clergy, or the school masters or even the parish clerk, and was undertaken in accordance with the rubric in the Order for the Visitation of the Sick in the Prayer Book.[5] Many copies of the Prayer Book that were printed in the seventeenth and eighteenth centuries contained the preamble to be used by those who were drawing up a will; included in this preamble were the hope of eternal life and instructions as to the disposal of his mortal remains.

One illustration of this practice is found in the will of Ralph Bamber in 1701. William Wood, the curate of Broughton, said in his evidence in the matter of this disputed will that 'he had received a summons to attend the sick man and draw up the will'. He continued, 'My duty as curate of the chapel of Broughton was to prevent a dispute after Ralph Bamber's death'. When he had drawn the will, he summoned Leonard Eccles and Edmund Daniels to witness the will, which 'they did by making their mark'.[6]

The operation of the custom of York is illustrated in the will of Abraham Sanderson of Thurlstone in 1652. After the preamble concerning his health, 'being weak of bodie but of perfect mind and memory praised be God . . .', and instructions for the disposal of his body, and the payment of his debts and also of his funeral expenses, he divided his estate into thirds.

I do hereby bequeath all right, title, clayme and demand which I have unto the messuages or Tenements called Cross Royd Head and Banckes House so I will a third thereof of all the edifices, buildings, barns, Foulds, orchards, gardens, Closes, lands, grounds and hereditaments whatsoever to the said third part of the said messuages . . . belonging unto Elizabeth Sanderson and Ann Sanderson my two elder daughters and to their heyres and assigns for ever being nowe in their minorities toward their maintenance and preferment and as concerning my personal estate in goods (the Rights of Anne my nowe wife for her third part thereof being deducted) I give and bequeath out of my

said goods tenne pounds in moneys to Mary Sanderson
my youngest daughter to be paid to her for her whole
Childes part and portion or to John Bamford my father
in law and grandfather to the said Mary as Tutor for
my said daughter Mary during her minority the said
tenne pounds to be paid . . . to my daughter Mary for
her maintenance and preferment by Elizabeth and Ann
Sanderson my above . . . daughters whom I make joynte
executrices of this my last will and testament to whom I
give and bequeath all my said goods and personal estate
. . . And I make and appoint William Riche of Hornefitt and
Ambrose Wordsworth . . . my loveing friends guardians
and Tutors for my two elder daughters and supervisors of
this my last will and testament . . .[7]

This will reveals something of the relationships within a small
community in South Yorkshire. Abraham Sanderson had no son,
only three daughters who were all minors. His father-in-law was
appointed guardian for the youngest daughter Mary, and his
close friends Ambrose Wordsworth and William Riche, both
important local gentry, were appointed as guardians for his
elder daughters because they would in due course be in a
position to obtain good preferment or advantages.

In theory the church was expected to administer the third
part of an intestate's estate by paying his debts and giving
support to some charity. However, the task was undertaken
by the church in a very haphazard manner: debts were not
always paid or donations given to charity. Naturally there were
many complaints, so Parliament, by the statute of Westminster
II (1285), appointed the bishop of a diocese to be responsible
for paying the debts of the deceased, in the same manner as an
executor had to do if the deceased had left a will. Also in the
case of a person who died intestate, the bishop was directed
to appoint 'the next and most lawful friends of the deceased'
to administer the estate.[8]

This arrangement was the origin of the office of administrator,
who became a court official. The control of the church over the
effects of a deceased person was thus reduced to the simple
administrative task of granting probate and issuing Letters of
Administration. By what means a person obtained the right to
make a full will is uncertain. Certainly it was not the direct

result of legislation but rather the emergence of a new custom which displaced a much older one only in the south but not in the north.

In the mid fourteenth century the old system of land tenure began to break down as England, very slowly, moved from a pastoral and agrarian economy towards a capitalist one. By 1530 a device had to be found that would enable a person to make a will that could include land. So the system emerged of creating 'uses' or trusts in a legal manner that could be enforced by chancery. The land for disposal was conveyed by the testator to trustees, who were known as 'feoffees to uses'. They disposed of the use of the land but not the land itself through the testator's will. So many abuses arose that Parliament resolved to put an end to these by passing the Statute of Uses (1536), which removed the legality of making a will by this means. The north resented this removal of the right, seeing it as a threat, and this objection became one of the grievances put forward by Robert Aske in the abortive Pilgrimage of Grace (1536).

The sequel to this opposition was the Statutes of Wills of 1540 and 1542, which enabled a testator to dispose of real property or land.[9] These Acts meant that there was for the future no necessity for two separate documents to a will, so the two were united into a single one beginning, 'This is the last Will and Testament of . . .'.

The Restoration Settlement of 1660 abolished the remnants of the feudal system of land tenure by making it possible to devise land by removing knight service and replacing it by the clause 'held in free and common socage as of our Manor of East Greenwich'. By this reform most land became devisable, so any will in which land was devised became a document of title which, prior to 1927, did not require probate.

The matter of settling the estates of those who died intestate was defined by the Statutes of Distribution of 1671 and 1685.[10] By and large these Statutes created schemes to enable the widow to claim one-third of the estate if there was a child, or one-half if there was no child or descendant of a child. Children took two-thirds if there was a widow, but failing that the children received equal shares of the entire estate. The descendants of such children as may have died in the lifetime of the intestate stood in the place of their parents. As time passed, ascendants, collaterals and half blood relationships were admitted according to the circumstances prevailing at the time.

Under common law a will could be either written out or spoken orally, which was known as a nuncupative will. Often these nuncupative wills were later committed to writing. If the will was not in writing, it had to be spoken orally by the testator in the presence of witnesses who had to record what was spoken. Nuncupative wills usually occurred when the testator had left the whole matter of his will until the very last moment when sickness had struck him down.[11]

An excellent example is the nuncupative will of William Whalley of Leeds shambles who died from the plague in 1648.

> The deceased published his will from his chamber window in the presence of us who stood in his court yard.[12]

During the seventeenth century, as prosperity tended to increase, more people began to make wills. This naturally led to a considerable amount of fraud taking place. To terminate this practice, Parliament took action and in 1671 passed the Statute of Frauds,[13] which required that all wills concerning land should be in writing and signed by the testator in the presence of 'three or four credible witnesses'; this remained the rule until the statute was amended in 1837.

The Act of 1692, which enabled any inhabitant of the northern province to bequeath all his goods away from his family, was passed in the interests of his younger children.[14] However, if a wife had received a marriage portion at the time of her wedding, she received no share of her husband's estate under the custom of York. The same rule applied to the heir at law, for he received the land of the deceased. This raises the question of the origin of the custom of York. Was it the result of the influence of the church, which was always strong in the north, for the church was regarded as the protector of widows and orphans? Further, there was a long-standing rivalry between Canterbury and York concerning the jurisdiction of Canterbury in the north. This was further complicated by the powerful bishops of Durham, who exercised a palatine jurisdiction over a large part of the northern province. Nevertheless, church influence does not provide a satisfactory answer for the long continuation of the custom of York.

It is debatable whether or not it is right and proper to give a man the power, from either spite or vanity, to deprive his wife and family and all who have a just claim upon him of all his property at his death and so disappoint the expectations of relatives which have quite naturally been formed. It was the existence of this kind of situation that led to numerous causes in the consistory court in which wills were contested.[15] In many rural areas wills were not always proved nor was probate obtained. Both archdeacons' and rural deans' court books record the names of persons who had failed to obtain probate and had proceeded to distribute the deceased's effects without lawful authority.[16]

3

PROBATE
AND ADMINISTRATION

During the middle ages the Church in England and Wales obtained the right, with certain exceptions, to prove the wills and grant letters of administration to the executors for the estates of all deceased persons; the exceptions were certain manorial courts and peculiar jurisdictions.

To the modern reader this may seem to have been a very odd situation, but it had advantages in that the medieval church could provide more efficient officers and courts to handle the business than any equivalent state agent or civil court was able to do at the time. The close connection between the church and the business of proving wills had important effects. In the first place, proving wills provided church officials with a good regular income from fees charged. Registering and storing wills with their inventories and executors' bonds involved a considerable amount of office work. On the whole this business was more profitable than the effort that was demanded in processing a cause through the consistory courts.

Since the correction courts of the archdeacons, and, in Chester, those of the rural deans, went on circuit through the deaneries, probate and administration could be handled at the same time. The revenue thus created helped to meet the overhead costs. The disadvantage to the church was its involvement in revealing illegal administration of the estates of the deceased. In those deaneries where the business was conducted in an efficient manner, additional odium was brought on the church courts.

The detection and reporting of offenders rested usually with the apparitors, those diocesan policemen who kept an eye not only on the clergy and laity, but also on the commissaries of the archdeacons, the dean and chapter courts at York and Durham, including those of the peculiar jurisdictions. As apparitors were paid solely by fees, the more offenders they could catch, the greater their income. The system was open to abuse by bribery, so it was often criticized in Puritan propaganda. A Puritan satirical poem of some length was produced as evidence in a consistory cause from Prestbury attacking court officers:

from Curates without consciences and parsons without wives,
from chydeing in the church & from dogged looks,
from talebearers, parritors and Bishoppes Bookes,
from the world and the flesh & the claws of old Nick,
Libera nos domine.[1]

In the same way as some twentieth-century policemen insist on observing the letter of the law without any leniency, so the seventeenth-century apparitors believed that the law must be obeyed to the letter. Hence they kept an eye on funerals in order to check that the widow duly took out letters of administration. They also listened to gossip in order to discover cases where illegal administration of a deceased person's estate had taken place and also the names of those who were cohabiting under the pretence of marriage.[2]

Once the funeral was over then application was made for the will to be authenticated by admission to probate or the award of letters of administration. If it was considered that the will might be contested, then a longer and more unchallengeable method was used known as 'probate in solemn form of law'. Otherwise the will was proved in 'common form' which was undertaken by the executors named in the will or the next of kin who took out letters of administration.

Travelling to an administrative centre to prove a will could be, in the dioceses of Chester and York, a traumatic experience, for both dioceses included within their boundaries extensive mountainous regions and areas of forest and marsh land traversed by very primitive roads. Henry Prescott describes his journey from Ashbourne (Derby) to Astbury on such roads in August 1708.

Mount about 4 in Moonshine, presently cross the River Dove, rise the mountains into the Morelands of Staffordshire, fall into difficult roads in a barren and wild country, the road falls down a steep rocky way to a dry Channel of rude and horrid aspect, after half a mile we meet the stream, falling at once out of sight under its bed or channel, proceed over wild Mores, a rude road uneven precipices after 4 hours at a good rate for the way, come to Leek 8 miles in their account. . . . We cross the Charnet at the Town enter into almost equall unpleasant roads ride by Horton . . . ascend the summit limitts of the Countys descend 2 miles and come (8 such miles) to Astbury.[3]

Such roads made it impossible for any individual who required probate or letters of administration to travel to York, Richmond or Chester to comply with the law. Hence the custom evolved in which probate 'in common form' was granted by the rural deans. This system became widespread in both dioceses and even in the city of York itself.

Employing rural deans in this manner was a natural thing to do because in the diocese of York they were episcopal officers who were removable at will and easily disciplined. Moreover, each rural dean had his own apparitor through whom orders could be executed. In the diocese of Chester, since the two archdeacons were titular officers only, the rural deans were the direct officers of the bishop and as such were appointed by letters patent, normally for life.[4] The Chester rural deans were given power to issue probate on the wills of all deceased persons in the diocese whose estates were less than £40, those of knights, esquires and clergy excepted. The wills of this latter group were proved by the commissaries of the Richmond or Chester archdeaconries.

Probate in common form could be challenged in the court at any time within ten years of the grant. If during this interval a witness died, no record of their evidence survived because the examination conducted by the rural dean was an oral one. The process for granting probate in common form was usually begun by the executor, and a formal citation was issued against all persons who claimed to have any interest in the estate. The person who would have the right to administer the estate, should probate fail, was always specifically named in the citation and ordered to be present when the will was proved. At that point, both the will and the inventory were exhibited in court, the witnesses sworn and the examination held privately by the rural dean or his deputy.[5]

If the will was contested, as indeed many were, a cause was opened in the consistory court in the same manner as any other cause in that court. When the hearing was concluded, the judge pronounced on the validity of the will or a codicil, a decision that could be challenged only by the process of an appeal to the provincial or chancery court at York.[6]

4

IN SICKNESS AND IN HEALTH

Life in the seventeenth century and for a great part of the eighteenth was uncertain in duration for a very large percentage of the population. Oliver Heywood, curate of Coley chapel in the parish of Halifax, in the latter half of the seventeenth century records in his diary that on the whole life was very insecure. Whenever he left Coley in order to visit his dissenting friends in Bolton, Bury, Rochdale or some of the West Riding towns and villages, he had no idea whether on his return he would find the family intact or learn that death had removed some of his own family, friends or neighbours during his absence.[1] Hence the frequent recourse to periods of fasting and long prayers in the hope that death might be averted.

Although the last serious outbreak of the plague had occurred in 1665, there were numerous other diseases that could terminate any person's life no matter what the age, sex or social standing of those afflicted. Society was preoccupied in that uncertain world with the danger of catching a cold, which could lead very quickly to a fever that ended in death. Even a simple cut on a finger could lead to death from blood poisoning. Naturally people worried about their coughs and the state of their bowels.

It is evident from reading the diary of Henry Prescott and other diaries of the same period that society on the whole was unhealthy. Very few families managed to live through a single year without one member suffering a serious illness. Living conditions in both the town and the country encouraged diseases that ended in death. Families lived in narrow, stinking streets, in airless houses with middens and privies that drained into wells from which people drew their drinking water. In rural areas, matters were little different: houses had adjacent privies, middens, pigsties and other animal houses from which effluent drained into wells and polluted the water.

Conditions of dirt and disease had been accepted as part of the life of the majority of ordinary folks further than the memory of man could extend. Not until the mid eighteenth century did doctors connect dirt with disease and with overcrowding, which intensified the problem. Even artisans and small tradesmen seldom occupied more than two rooms in a house and rented out the remainder. In towns such as Manchester and Liverpool, cellar dwellings were common and these damp and insanitory rooms were all too often the source of fevers.

So long as life remained precarious then sickness could and did result in death. Disease carried away more people than ever died from natural causes. Long after the plague had disappeared from England, influenza, typhoid fever and even measles could be fatal. Parish registers often record the cause of death and these registers reveal the extent to which smallpox, measles, whooping cough and scarlet fever were the scourges in many towns.

The registers of the parish of St Mary, Castlegate, York, reveal the ravages of disease especially amongst children. The following extracts for August 1785 illustrate the scourge of smallpox:

Aug.2 William Headley s of William Headley, Labourer, Far Water Lane died July 31, age 3 yrs small pox.
5th Elizabeth d. John Douglas, Joiner, Far Water Lane, died Aug.3 age 2 yrs, small pox
6th John s John Boys Labourer, Middle Lane died Aug.4 age 2 yrs, small pox
9 Mary d John Mare, Comb Maker, Middle Lane died Aug.8, age 2 yrs small pox
18 Francis s John Prest, Waterman, died Aug 16 age 10 months small pox.[2]

This outbreak of smallpox, which carried off ninety children under 5 years of age, was by no means an isolated incident, in either towns or villages. During the years 1782, 1784 and 1785 the disease was extensively prevalent in the north. Cornelius Ashworth, clothier of Soyland in Halifax, recorded in his diary some details of the outbreak of the disease in Halifax in 1782.

29 December. I went to Halifax, heard Mr Knight preach. I saw 10 open graves in the church yard, 9 of them for Children & was informed that 110 Children had been interred in the graveyard in 4 weeks which died of smallpox.[3]

Henry Prescott, deputy Registrar of Chester, records in his diary for 1710 the death of his old friend Mr Davies, one of the proctors in the consistory court.

8 July. Mr Davies dies about 9 this morning, after 12 days affected with the small pox. So good and learned a person falls not unlamented by mankind in concern, the shock to his Family . . . is great, amazeing, not curable but by the gentle Application of time and patient submission to the Almighty hand.[4]

Most people recognized that time was a great healer when death struck and that the hand of God was in all things. However, taking all things into consideration, it was believed that good fortune and a sound constitution enabled some people to join the select company of those who managed to survive into advanced old age. One such was Henry Prescott's godmother, Ann Rigby, whom he went to visit on 25 May 1717 at Upholland near Wigan.

About 4 in a soft rain, set out, got thoro Holland . . . wait on my Godmother Rigby now tho' very old and advancing near 90, very apprehensive and of a cheerful humour . . . speaking of her own lean hand . . . said, 'Cozen, I have but little food for the worms.'[5]

No doubt it passed through Henry's mind that she was thinking of her approaching end, which could not be long delayed.

The survival of a great deal of folklore and folklore remedies in sickness, which eighteenth-century enthusiasts found most helpful, certainly assisted in effecting cures. Henry Prescott records in his diary that he had frequent recourse to such items as snail water, sage tea, wormwood and the ever-popular Daffy's Elixir. This was a remedy of the mid seventeenth century that was composed of brandy, canary wine, oranges, lemons and rhubarb, to which was added a little borax in order to convince the customer that it was not an expensive form of gin.

As the years passed, other cordials were tried on the advice of friends. On 7 April 1717, Henry Prescott wrote, 'I took

Mr White's Bitter Snake root which cost me one shilling and sixpence.' On the 24th of the same month he notes that he took the advice of Dr Holbrook, Warden of Manchester Collegiate Church, who told him to drink Scarborough water. This northern spa was becoming a popular resort and the curative properties of its spa water were widely advertised.

Moderation in eating and drinking was not regarded as a virtue at this time and Henry Prescott, like so many of his contemporaries, was no exception. On the occasion of his visit to Blackburn to see the widow of the former vicar and rural dean on 29 May 1708 he noted in his diary: 'come to Blackburn about 3, very thirsty and weary. Sup on Mrs Price's good mutton and fat capon.' A rich meal late in the evening was succeeded by the inevitable restless night, for on the following day he recorded that 'After Elixir and secure repose revived, apply to Busienes'.[6]

Individuals made every effort to avert death by taking a variety of remedies, for interest in medicine was not confined to the professionals. John Archer, writing in 1673, indicated that every man was trying to be his own doctor.[7] One Dudley Ryder in his diary advocated regular visits to the cold bath, which he believed would 'strengthen my body, purge it of ill humours, fence me against the cold, prevent convulsions, secure me against the gout'.[8]

Certainly, Henry Prescott followed this advice when he travelled with Bishop Dawes and a group of friends to visit Chatsworth, Nottingham, and the great houses of the Dukeries. He gives details about the problems of travel and the precautions to be taken when arriving drenched to the skin at Bakewell, after crossing the Derbyshire moors.

> . . . thence over Buxton Moor . . . all in a wild and uneven road to Buxton: about 12 a clock, Mr Egerton, the Doctor, Mrs Legh, Shalcross, Downes, Jodrel, myself and Jack go into the cold bath, swim and divert 1/2 an hour . . . We hasten to Buxton, take the remains of a dinner, after . . . Mrs Egerton comes hither in all 42. A brisk shower falls, we mount in it and it is about constant over the Moors, 8 miles to Bakewell where wee come steep'd about 7 to the Red Lyon. Common application is made to avoid any danger from the rain.[9]

The common application was usually a gill of brandy, which was his favourite drink and one which he took on every convenient occasion.

Those who could afford the cost went to Bath, the most famous of English spa towns at this period. One who went for the cure was the Revd Charles Sampson, vicar of Ripley, who wrote to the bishop of Chester about his long absences from his benefice. The reasons he gives reveal how devastating a severe illness could be: 'I left Ripley last year with my wife & children in consequence of a very severe attack in my head which . . . so affected my eyes that I was under the necessity of wearing a bandage over them.' The journey to Bath was interrupted by a series of fits that affected his second son so seriously that the family began to despair of his life. Having recovered from these, the family was beginning to feel better when a second disaster struck. The second son became the victim of whooping cough 'and at the interval of a fortnight . . . was caught by our two younger boys, (the youngest only eight months old)'.

No sooner had this infection begun to clear and the family expected to return to Ripley than Sampson was summoned to London on business that detained him in the city for five weeks. Sampson had only just returned to Bath when a third blow struck the family:

a putrid sore throat brought one of our children into a very alarming state & spread in my family. My wife was infected by it & in consequence of that . . . & agitation of mind resulting from her attendance on our children, a miscarriage at a very precarious time . . . took place in December.

Her recovery took far longer than was anticipated because she suffered from weakness and depression. Charles Sampson had now no alternative but to ask the bishop to extend his leave of absence from his parish in order to avoid the penalties of the Act concerning the non-residence of the clergy.[10]

Little wonder need be expressed at discovering that persons afflicted by a range of diseases sought new cures. By the early eighteenth century other cures were being introduced. The ever-popular seventeenth-century cure of Daffy's Elixir had a rival in the Queen of Hungary's water, which was basically rosemary flavoured with brandy, 'a spoonfull taken when feeling run down night or day ad libitum'.[11] On 28 June

1707, Henry Prescott tried out Saughton's Drops in spring water. Another innovation was the introduction of eastern drugs on a large scale, especially opium. This drug was used in the manufacture of Sydenham's Laudanum, to which was added saffron, cinnamon and cloves in a pint of canary wine, and this became the eighteenth-century equivalent of the modern aspirin. Treacle water was considered to be a universal remedy against every possible disease. Further, there is evidence that the York doctors were, at this period, recommending the smoking of cannabis as a cure for headaches.[12]

Many of the medicines offered by doctors were patently absurd, with the result that a great deal of magic and astrology was practised. Charms and amulets were sold in large quantities, while the publishers of popular almanacks gave information as to the most propitious time for medical treatment. John Webster, writing in 1677, records how he dealt with those who believed they were 'bewitched, forespoken, blasted or fairy taken':

> If you indulge their fancy, and seem to concurr in opinion with them and hang any insignificant thing about their necks assuring them that it is a most efficacious charm, you may easily settle their imagination and give them that which is proper to eradicate their disease.[13]

On the whole, taking into consideration the state of medicine, the charm could be more effective in effecting a cure than the doctor.

During the seventeenth century, surgeons increased their skill and physicians prescribed bleeding, but they considered it to be beneath their dignity to administer the cure themselves, although there is evidence in Henry Prescott's diary to the contrary.[14] On the other hand, apothecaries were now rising to the rank of doctor. Their training took eight years, during which time they became skilled in the use and application of an extensive range of drugs and herbs. Lady Mary Wortley, writing in 1749, was very critical of the doctors of her day:

> When I recollect the vast fortunes raised by doctors amongst us and the eager pursuit after every new piece that is introduced, I cannot help thinking that there is a fund of credulity in mankind, that must be employed

somewhere, and the money formerly given to the monks for the health of the soul is now thrown to the doctors for the health of the body and generally with as little real prospect of success.[15]

An insight is provided into medical practice by the case of the Revd William Dennis, rector of Doddleston, who caught a fever from the severe drenching he received during a storm on his return journey from Lancaster. He soon became delerious and was attended by the doctor Henry Williamson who, by the close of 1695, declared him to be cured. However, Dennis's brain continued to be in a state of confusion, 'being afflicted with a deep Melancholy which was increased and heightened by having a Sonn of his runaway ... to be a soldier in Flanders'. Three years later, Dennis fell from his horse on to his head, receiving a serious injury which produced the following result:

> sometimes hee has been Frantick, att other times so melancholy that hee has sitten whole days together & would not speak a word ... sometimes sing strange Rhymes part English, part Latin of his own composition extempore.

Further, Dennis became addicted to pipe smoking and Dr Williamson believed that he had contracted Synochus Putrida as a result of his failure to take the necessary precautions following his drenching in the storm. The symptons included a most peculiar hiccough which was accompanied by 'perpetual ravings and a clammy coldness of the lower parts. I gave him a sharp glister by which ... he ejected many yellow, greenish fetid humors which caused him to faint.'[16] In the end, Dr Wiliamson failed to effect a complete cure so that Dennis had no alternative other than to resign his living.

Venereal disease was an affliction that could very easily end in death. Those who contracted this disease aroused as much fear amongst the residents of their communities as do those who are afflicted with the HIV virus today. In 1664 William Halliwell was involved in a defamation cause against Peter Leigh, accusing the latter of contracting the pox during the time they were apprentice glovers in Dublin.

One morning Halliwell and his fellow apprentice Cook went into Leigh's bedroom where he showed them 'his swollen member', and requested the services of a surgeon. Leigh and Cook found a surgeon who, being informed of the nature of the case, refused to attend, saying 'he would not meddle with the case'. Eventually the two were put into contact with a Mr Bell, a barber surgeon, who came and dressed the affected part, commenting that 'he had only arrived just in time', for any further delay would have meant death.[17]

These barber surgeons dealt with cases that doctors refused to handle. They also undertook bleeding or cupping as an addition to their usual trade of cutting hair, shaving, extracting teeth and making wigs.

There were apothecaries who provided cordials to enable a woman to procure an abortion arising from an unwanted pregnancy. In 1677 Margaret Royden, fearing that her indiscretion had led to a pregnancy, drank a potion composed of bearsfoot and water germander (black helibore), which, it was said, 'would make a mare drop its foal and a woman her child'. It was well known in 1612 that there was an apothecary in Warrington who made up such potions and sold them to the public.[18] Since black helibore is a poison, there was always the risk of death arising from its consumption, which undoubtedly happened on occasion to the woman who drank it. Apothecaries were believed to make very high profits, yet they never appear to have made fortunes since the majority died before the age of 50.

The vulnerable members of society appear to have been those in their twenties and thirties or even forties who were actively engaged in running a business or manufacturing goods and bringing up a family at the same time. The death of the male head of a family in his prime was an unmitigated disaster that struck quite frequently. Having depended upon his earnings for the support of the family, the widow and children had to be provided for, hence the harrowing scenes that sometimes took place around the deathbed.

Taking into consideration both the short- and long-term effectiveness of the wide variety of medical treatment, the result in the long term was always death; that final act in the drama of life.

5

DEATH AND BURIAL

Throughout countless centuries death has been a subject for comment. The Roman poet Horace depicts death as a silent figure moving steadily from place to place and house to house:

> Pale death with measured step
> Strikes at the cottages of the poor,
> And the mansions of the great.[1]

Francis Bacon, writing his essay on the subject of death in 1625, refers to death as a fear, full of foreboding and dread.

> Men fear death as children fear to go in the dark: and as that natural fear in children is increased with tales, so is the other.[2]

It was generally agreed that the psalmist had correctly defined man's allotted span, as mourners listened to the reciting of psalm 90 in the burial office:

> The days of our age are three score years and ten: and though men be so strong that they come to four score years, yet is their strength but labour and sorrow, so soon passes it away and we are gone.[3]

The great mass of the population were uneducated, yet even those who were able to read would get no further than reading the tracts sold by street hawkers. Written in lurid and sentimental language, these printed accounts went into great detail concerning the violent and tragic deaths of the victims. Hell was a reality at this period, and the fear of having to face it was increased by the highly coloured language that was

26

used to describe the terrors that awaited sinners. The popular literature of the period reflects the theme of death as a direct punishment for sin.[4] Publications giving detailed accounts of violent deaths became very popular, such as 'the execution of six young criminals', the gay yet tragic story of the two Swiss soldiers, or 'the peasant who by his death made his wife and children happy' and the 'fatal wedding night', and numerous other stories in like vein.[5]

By the mid eighteenth century the concept of Hell had changed. Excessive fear had led to incredulity, so Hell was not so much rejected as transformed into a literary fashion. It became clear that, when men learned to reject the apprehension of eternal punishment, the progress of what were regarded as impiety and immorality had been very considerable. Although the rejection of Hell eased the pain of death and the act of dying, nevertheless the eighteenth-century attitude to death supports the general hypothesis that the doctrinal and religious changes of the Reformation had little actual effect on a community's reactions to death and burial. This is very true of the rural and remote parts of the northern dioceses, especially the western part of the diocese of York, where old traditions lingered on long after other parts of the country had discarded them.

It was the feeling of loss rather than the concept of an afterlife that dominated and shaped the response to death and bereavement. John Moor, writing in 1617, stated that:

> Everyone feareth the death of the body but few are afraid of the death of the soul. That which cannot be avoided men seek to shun; but to avoid sin (that they may live for ever) few or none do care.[6]

By the close of the eighteenth century, death was an even greater trauma for the bereaved and this was especially true of infant and child mortality. The rapidly expanding population in the new industrial towns, who lived in some appalling conditions, saw child deaths multiply, as the parish registers of these towns reveal. Some Victorian novelists were affected by this attitude towards death and wrote lurid accounts of the dying person groaning in agony and suffering convulsions, with discoloured features, while their relatives, family and friends grouped round the deathbed wearing heavy black clothing. Such accounts were often concluded by giving extremely gloomy details of the funeral, all of which only served to present death as a truly terrible event.

On the other hand, Henry Prescott could comment quite calmly upon the death of his youngest child, Suzy, in 1708: 'This morning about 2 my youngest child Suzy, after a great weakness with Convulsions for near three weeks together, leads this troublesome Candidate, I hope to a better life.'[7] Prescott faced the approaching death of his relatives and friends with equanimity. In March 1709 Henry and his wife, Susannah, set out from Chester to visit his mother-in-law Puleston in Wrexham who was seriously ill. In this connection, Prescott could write, 'My Suzy and I set for Wrexham about 10. I see my mother Puleston, shee is very weak, apprehensive of her change, cheerfully submitting.'[8] In contrast, he expressed deep concern for the state of his cousin Gerard Eyton, with whom he had financial dealings: 'Wee visit Gerard Eyton, wee find him weak macerated, tormented with a cough and his next relations in deep apprehension and concern about him, but wee see no violent symtons.'[9]

In a similar vein Sarah Smyter wrote about sickness to her brother Henry Gambier:

> Dear Brother, I was very sorry to hear of you being so bad but rejoysed very much in your next to hear of your being like to do well again . . . I was so bad myself that I thought I should have deighed; I was took with a violent chollick in my stomach which held me from Satterday to Thursday.
>
> I have had the misfortune of losing my deare child Johney, he deyd last week of a feaver . . . it is a great trouble to me but these misfortunes we must submit two.[10]

In the majority of cases the final stage before death is described in identical words to those used in the case of Thomas Benson of Claughton in 1723, 'being weak & infirm in body and sick of his last sickness'.[11]

If it should happen that both parents died within a short time of each other, then relatives would be appointed as guardians of the children in order to protect family interests on one side. An excellent example of this occured in a cause brought by Francis and Rebecca Grosvenor of Ireland and William and Martha Mason against John Seacombe, who was appointed a guardian of Robert Seacombe, heir to a considerable amount of property in Liverpool.[12] This matter will be discussed later.

Not every appointment of a guardian to a minor was a trustworthy person and certain to be reliable. Agnes Lorymar of Lamplugh took action against Antony Patrickson who had taken her nephew Richard Hunterlow into his care. Agnes became suspicious of Patrickson's motives, so she made up her mind to obtain custody of her nephew, 'being at underage from her and she did not know what had become of him'. According to her deposition, Agnes went to Stockhome, the house of Anthony Patrickson, 'fearing that some harm was or might befall him, nor would Antony Patrickson tell her what had become of him'. Upon his refusal, Agnes adopted the age-old custom of uttering a solemn cursing of Patrickson by 'kneeling at his house upon her knees and praid God that a vengeance might light upon him'.[13] This action terrified Patrickson, who promptly returned the boy to his aunt.

In the event of the widow entering upon a second marriage then there were further tensions, as will be noted later, that could lead to expensive court actions.

The sad scenes around the deathbed were quickly forgotten in the preparations for the burial, reading the will and discussing the division of the deceased's money and effects between his heirs.

Funerals could be expensive occasions. From time to time the authorities attempted to control costs by fixing legal costs, limiting these to a shroud, a coffin, the cost of digging the grave, the fees for tolling the passing bell, the fee to the incumbent for the burial office, fees to the parish clerk and the pall bearers. No funeral ornaments were to be permitted and the total cost was not to exceed 40 shillings. This rule was frequently broken; many families had costly funerals with ornaments and trappings.[14]

When a person was seen to be approaching death, it was the custom to toll the church bell, or 'ring the knell' as it was called, to announce to the neighbourhood that a member of the community was close to death. Immediately death took place, a relative was sent to notify the sexton or parish clerk to toll the passing bell so that the parishioners would know that a death had taken place and the age of the deceased. The passing bell consisted of nine strokes or 'trailers' for a man, six for a woman and three for a child, followed by a single stroke for each year of the deceased's life.

It was the passing bell that inspired John Donne to comment in his *Devotions*:

> Who bends not his ear to any bell which upon any occasion rings? But who can remove it from that bell which is passing a piece of himself out of this world? No man is an Island, entire of it self; every man is a piece of the Continent, a part of the main; if a clod be washed away by the sea, Europe is the less, as well as if a promontory were, as well as if a manor of thy friends or of thine own were; any man's death diminishes me, because I am involved in Mankind; and therefore never send to know for whom the bell tolls; It tolls for thee.[15]

Bells were also tolled when a body was carried through another parish or chapelry on its way to be interred in the parish churchyard. This was the custom in Halifax until 1676 when the chapel of Illingworth was allowed to bury in the chapel yard; previously the dead were carried 4 miles from Illingworth to Halifax for burial.[16]

Henry Prescott recorded the announcement of the death of Bishop Nicholas Stratford on 16 February 1706/7: 'I receive Letters from Dr and Mr Stratford giving the sad Account that my Lord dy'd about Noon on Wednesday. The great Bell tolls the unwelcome News to the City.'[17]

At death, the corpse was handed over to the women whose profession it was to wash the body and prepare it for burial. The body was then laid out in a ground-floor room and shrouded, but not always placed in a coffin. Many parishes had a parish coffin in which to convey the corpse to the grave, for poor people were unable to afford the cost of a coffin. The depressed state of the textile trade in the 1670s saw an Act passed by Parliament to make burial in a woollen shroud compulsory. Five yards of cloth were to be used for the shroud under a penalty of £5 for failing to comply. Since those who failed to comply with the Act could be informed upon, and the informer could receive half the penal sum as a reward, it became the custom to send a relative to inform the incumbent that burial in a woollen shroud would not take place, so the real cost was reduced to 50 shillings.[18]

Alexander Pope in his poem, *Epistle to Lord Cobham*, pokes fun at burials in woollen cloth:

> 'Odious! in woollen! 'twould a saint provoke!'
> (were the last words that poor Narcissa spoke)
> 'No, let a charming chintz, and Brussels lace,
> Wrap my cold limbs and shade my lifeless face:
> One would not, sure, be frightful when one's dead:
> And – Betty – give this cheek a little red.'[19]

In some houses the clocks were stopped at the hour of death, mirrors were covered and pictures either turned to the wall or covered with a very thick black cloth. The corpse was kept in the house for three days at least to ensure that the deceased was not alive and so avoid the risk of their being buried alive.

Invitations were delivered orally to friends and relatives of the deceased to attend the funeral – a custom that survived in the West Riding of Yorkshire and other northern areas until the 1940s.[20] Six of the deceased person's closest friends were invited to act as bearers to carry the coffin to the church and then to the grave. This act of friends carrying the deceased signifies the solidarity of the dead with the living.

Henry Prescott records the funeral of his mother-in-law Puleston at Wrexham on 27 March 1709: 'about 1/2 hour after 4 this evening dies, that very tender, charitable and religious person, My good mother Puleston.' Three days later he gives an account of her funeral:

> About 2, I set for Wrexham, come hither about 4. The company comes with leasure and makes up a considerable number. About 6 the Funeral then proceeds without pomp or indeed the decent solemnities due to the merit and quality of the person. She is interr'd close to the north wall . . . Mr Price [the vicar] performing the Office.[21]

Mourners were always dressed in black, with the female relatives wearing black veils, while the men wore hats with black crepe bands. Mourning periods were lengthy: parents wore black for six months; this was reduced to eighteen weeks for grandparents and a mere eight weeks for a brother or sister.

The funeral procession was drawn up in strict order, with the immediate relatives walking behind the coffin, followed by more distant relatives and finally the friends of the family. Before leaving for the church, wine and finger biscuits were handed out to the mourners.

The corpse was met at the church gate by the officiant, who preceded it into the church. If the deceased was in Holy Orders, the coffin was placed in the chancel facing west, but a layman or woman's coffin was placed at the upper end of the nave facing east. If the deceased happened to be an important citizen or an ecclesiastical officer or member of a cathedral chapter, then a eulogy would be read in their honour. When the burial office was ended, the coffin or, if there was no coffin, the body was carried to the grave, preceded by the officiant, and lowered into it. Earth was then thrown upon the coffin with the mourners grouped around. When all was concluded the principal mourners returned to the house for a funeral meal followed by the reading of the will.

Henry Prescott describes the funeral of his cousin Gerard Eyton on 3 August 1715:

> Wee call at Chris. Meredith's, thence to my cozn Eyton where wee find the company thickening to the Funeral of my cozn Gerard Eyton (who dy'd Thursday last). After a full and hansom refreshment the company of Mourners and Bearers settled. A great company of Horse, Foot and 4 Coaches move after 3 which is increas'd at Bangor.
>
> Hee is interr'd about 6. After the solemnity a good company (12 at the least) is invited and generously entertained with very good Ale and Beer by Mr Jones.[22]

The right to an exclusive burial place within a church was a right that was jealously guarded, and causes were often brought into the consistory court to prohibit anyone from obstructing or infringing this right. One cause relating to this right came from Bolton in 1701. It concerned the burial place of the Lever family of Little Lever, on the grounds that the churchwardens intended to erect a staircase to the new gallery, which would mean placing the base of the staircase over the burial place. The judge gave sentence that the proposals for a fixed staircase should be withdrawn and replaced by 'a moveable pair of stairs upon the Buryall place under them and that they be removed when so required at no charge to those to whom the Gallery is granted'.[23] This sentence cleared the pew owners in the gallery from any liability for paying the cost of removing and replacing the staircase when required.

Another method of protecting burial rights in a church was to petition for a faculty to enable a pew or pews to be erected over the vault. In 1718 Sergius Halsall, Gilbert Taylor and Edward Ashcroft, husbandmen of Ormskirk, claimed title to a 'certain plot of ground for burial lying near to the North Church Door of the parish church'. The petitioners wanted the right to erect separate seats over the burial place for their own private use on the assumption that, 'Mr Halsall hath for many years past and still does faithfully promise at his Death if he dye unmarried (or without issue of his body) That he will give some credible gift or legacy to the use of the said church'.[24]

From time to time a yeoman would ask for burial next to his late wife. John Billington of Ashton, who died in 1672, said, 'being somewhat weak of body and going into ould years and taking some thoughts of the shortness of my life, I will that my body be buried at Weaverham in or near the place where my wife was layd in decent manner'.[25]

There are instances where the churchwardens were most concerned about certain families who were allowed to inter members in the chancel of a church but failed to make any contribution towards the cost of repairing it. One such was the Vaudrey family of St Olave's parish, Chester, which over the years had brought many suits before the consistory court concerning their title to bury in the chancel. The churchwardens, who were naturally anxious to recover some of their costs, decided to introduce fees for burials in the chancel, which were known as 'laystalls'. This charge was important for the churchwardens of St Olave's since the Vaudrey family had neglected to repair their chancel. Therefore the levying of laystalls provided a fund which could be utilized to cover the cost of repairs to the chancel.

One result of a family feud that had taken place was the decision by the Vaudreys to dispose of the family house in Chester. In 1684, Richard and Henry Vaudrey, sons of John Vaudrey, sold the house to Hugh Harvey, who made the request that, having acquired the Vaudrey house, and therefore also the right to be buried in the chancel of St Olave's, he and his family might be exempt from the payment of laystalls. His claim was based on the fact that, following the siege of Chester during the Civil War, he had found the chancel of St Olave's a ruin and repaired it at his own expense of 47s. 6d.[26] His request was granted.

As the seventeenth century drew towards its close, one aim comes to the fore. That was the desire to separate the living from the dead, which meant in reality the prohibition of burials within the church – a tendency that was very slow to be accepted as the norm in the northern province. Only very slowly did the graveyard become the recognized place for burials. The intention behind this change was to emphasize the difference between the two states of life and death.

Funerals have always reflected the social standing in a parish of those who died. Several factors influenced the relationship between the bereaved and the funeral rites. For the majority, canon law decided the actual burial itself, but the most powerful influence was that of tradition and custom on burial practices, which were, in time, modified by changing attitudes and circumstances. If the deceased was an important member of the community, then the funeral was on a grand scale, with horses, carriages, hatchments and other funeral gear.

An excellent illustration of this custom is to be found in Henry Prescott's account of the funeral of his great friend Lady Shackerley, a prominent figure in Chester society, at the close of the seventeenth century. The journey from Chester to Lower Peover chapel, including the burial office and eulogy, took some ten hours.

> Rise early and prepare for Attendance at Lady Shackerley's Funeral, go down to the House before 7. Not without sensible reflections on a Life of 58 years, observe and contemplate on the Melancholy solemnity. I meet with Alderman P. Bennett and Mr Sam Taylor in the Company, compare and find our ages concurr within or near a Year.

Conversations at funerals appear to have changed but little, since mourners today still exchange details concerning their ages. Prescott goes on to describe the funeral itself:

> At 9 the Herse moves forward attended thoro the Town by about 100 horse. At Tarvin the Number reduced to a very few beside the Mourners, a cool gale makes the journey tolerable and (saving the occasion) pleasant. About a mile

short of Midlewich, refresh on venison pasty and cold meat
prepar'd. Here the body taken into a room hung with Black
and lightn'd with wax candles, this pensive solemnity lasts
not 3 hours: before 5 wee proceed and come to Lower
Peover chapel about 6.

Prescott followed his narrative by commenting upon the burial
office and the eulogy, which he considered fell far short of what
Lady Shackerley deserved.

The service begun by Mr Yates. The Curat of Gresford has
a sermon. (Let me dy the death of the righteous and let
my last end be like his). Hee gives a plain substancial
Character of the good Lady thoro the several stages of her
Life, Youth, marriage, widowhood, which did not exceed
or reach her merit. Since I had the Honour to know her
in all the stages. I was extremely affected with an esteem
of her memory, other thoughts naturally arising from the
loss of a valuable person & the consideration of my own
Mortality. . . . The solemnity over about 7.

The funeral party then called at the vicarage expecting Mr Yates
to provide some good wine, but they were disappointed, for
Prescott commented that it was dull.[27]

When death involved a diocesan bishop then the funeral was
on a really magnificent scale. Bishop Nicholas Stratford died in
Oxford on 12 February 1706 and the funeral was arranged for
the 21st in Chester cathedral. Henry Prescott was present and he
recorded a detailed account of the event. Both he and Mr Cooper,
a proctor, spent so much time drinking mulled sack that they
were late for meeting the cortège and had to take a short-cut
through Mr Dawson's grounds.

The Herse, Coach and Undertakers sett hence about 6.
Mr Cooper and I stay and refresh in mull'd sack. . . .
Wee follow after 7 and overtake the Herse etc, near
the Plume of Feathers. Wee are readily admitted thoro
Mr Dawson's ground. Mr Cooper and I call on him, hee
gives us excellent Ale. Wee come to the Glass House about
1. Send a messenger to the City, upon which Coaches and
Company come to a great Number. Gloves are dealt to all
and Hatbands to particulars, Scarfs to a very few, myself

of this number. Past 3 put into order, wee proceed to the Barrs, here the Corporacion and Clergy serv'd with gloves etc., are ready. I dismount and walk on the side of the Clergy. The Herse and Funeral proceeds, the day very clear and calm in good order. At the Hall, the Corps are taken out of the Herse, the Coffin remarkably grave & rich & cover'd with velvet and gilt plates. 6 Bearers, 3 of which noble Clergymen attend; it proceeds to the Quire thoro the Broad Isle and a vast concourse. Mr Subdean Wright reads the prayers, Mr Lancaster the Lessons. The Dean has a Sermon, too little heard, on Dan.12 v 3. The Quire hung in great solemnity and crowded with great affection. About 6 the Office is over, the singing was not commended.[28]

The black hangings remained in the choir until the enthronement of his successor, Sir William Dawes, almost a year later.[29]

The funeral solemnities being concluded, Prescott and Canon Stratford, the late bishop's son, returned to the palace to read the will and prepare the formalities for handing over the spiritualities of the see to Archbishop Sharp of York until a successor had been elected.

Funeral customs, many dating from pre-Reformation times, survived in many parts of the north until the industrial revolution and the growth of urban communities destroyed them. It was the custom to place a cross on the corpse when carrying it to the church and this cross was composed of two towels laid crosswise on the bier. The Puritan clergy tried to suppress this as superstitious and popish. An example of this comes from Ribchester where the new vicar had attempted to reform his parishioners but without much success.

In 1639 Robert Abbott of Ribchester was cited to appear before the consistory court on the grounds that he maintained popish practices.

> . . . that you Robert Abbott accompanying the said Corps of Alice Leaver, the wyfe of Richard Leaver of Alston in Ribchester parish, who had not attended the parish church for 7 years, accompanied the corps where there was a Crosse towell layd over her Corps upon the Beare and she was sett downe at Stone and Wooden Crosses by the way and you did at the same Crosse in a superstitious

manner take off your hatt and kneeled down and prayed. And many people which saw you do think that you did worship and pray unto the Crosses.

Although the vicar of Ribchester, Mr Hindley, said that he had tried to reform Abbott's idolatry, it was to no avail, for in a spirited defence Abbott stated that:

A Towell was laid along the Corps and another less Towell was pinned over it to kepe the long one from flying off and not in any superstitious sort. And the corps was set downe at the Crosses and he amongst others took off his hat and said the Lord's Prayer.

Abbott admitted that he and Mr Hindley were in some disagreement since the vicar said he lied and was a knave, while Abbott cared nothing at all for the vicar and his remarks.[30] A similar incident took place in 1613 at Grinton in north Yorkshire when Richard Parke brought his mother's body to the church for burial with a 'suspicious Crosse laid over her'. Two other persons, Charles Hutchinson and John Metcalf, followed the same practice.[31] Since northern parishes were often very large in extent and the distance to the parish church for burial so long, it was essential for resting places to be available because the coffin had to be carried on the shoulders of the bearers. The custom of keeping a wake or watch by the dead body had almost died out in the south by 1600, but Archbishop Grindal, when at York in 1575, complained about the survival of old custom.[32] Mr Mawtese described a Yorkshire wake to John Aubrey at the close of the seventeenth century:

At the funerals in Yorkshire, to this day, they continue the custom of watching and sitting up all night till the body be interred. In the interim some kneel down and pray (by the corpse), some play at cards, some drink and take tobacco: they have also mimical plays and sports e.g. they choose a simple young fellow to be a judge, then the suppliants (having first blacked their hands by rubbing them under the bottom of a pot) beseech his Lordship and smut all his face.[33]

The glebe terriers for the parish of Sedbergh and its chapels of Garsdale and Dent record that fees were payable to the vicar of Sedbergh for every wake held in the two chapels, being 'fourpence for every night wake'.[34]   Although recusants were refused the right of burial in an Anglican churchyard, yet many such took place secretly by night, and there are many cases recorded in the Visitation Act books for the Archdeaconry of Richmond. Catherine Coates of Marrick, a recusant who died in 1618, was buried by night in the hopes of avoiding detection and reporting.[35]

The corpse of a suicide could not be legally buried in consecrated ground, but there are instances of people who committed suicide being buried in the night. In 1624, John Hannard dug a grave in the churchyard of Bolton on Swale and at night buried his brother Thomas, 'the same who did untimely put himself away'.[36]

Occasionally a person would refuse to have the burial office recited at a funeral. In 1696, Thomas Ashton refused to allow the vicar of Winwick, Thomas Waring, to officiate at the funeral of his wife Ellen. The vicar took the case to the consistory court where he said that on 5 January 1696 he went to the gate 'at the west end of the churchyard to meet the corpse and began to read the burial office'. Thomas Ashton, being one of the bearers with 'other accomplices in this unfair & contemptuous action', refused to obey the vicar and to enter the church, 'or give any attendance to the service'. Ashton, acting as spokesman, said to Waring, 'We are come to bury our Dead'. Replying, Waring said that their action was an 'interruption and disturbance of him in the execution of his office.' Thomas Ashton then carried the corpse to the grave, put it in and hastily covered it with earth without any office, in contempt of the Liturgy.[37]

Opposition existed to the custom of bringing the corpse of a close relative to the parish church for burial. In these cases it is usually an indication of dissent and rejection of the services of the Anglican Church. Interments in these cases took place elsewhere, usually in orchards, gardens or even fields.

In 1664, William Houldsworth of Wakefield was presented by the churchwardens to the Archdeacon of York on the grounds that he had buried his wife in a garden, as were Richard Marshall for burying his mother and John Wilkinson for burying his child, 'both in gardens'.[38] In the same year, John Metcalfe of Askrigg, who was a Quaker, refused to allow his late wife to be 'decently buried after the Order of the Church' but took her to the Quaker burial ground.[39]

The court books of the archdeacons of York and the commissaries of Richmond and Chester contain abundant examples of burials in unconsecrated ground. In 1677, Henry Wadsworth of Luddenden buried his daughter in 'an Horchard or Garth'.[40] Two years later, James Parkin of Gilling, aided and abetted by his wife Elizabeth, 'buryed his father, late of Burghead in his close called Mossdill Inge'.[41]

From time to time, when burials had to take place before or after divine service on Sunday, attempts were made to bypass the burial office by interring before the office could be recited. An instance of this arose in Hull in 1680 when the three friends of Richard Barnes 'forcibly opened the church doors and buried the corpse before the service appointed could begin'.[42]

Not all those who died were able to ensure that their mortal remains would be allowed to rest in peace. Certainly in one case from Wakefield, in 1687, William Hague and Joshua Norton were charged with having disturbed a grave: 'that they did take up the corpse of Joshua Shipley who had but lain in the grave two years and a month and abusing his body by cutting it in pieces.'[43] Taken in a literal manner, this incident could mean that the predecessors of Jeremiah Cruncher in the *Tale of Two Cities* were at work in 1687 when interest in anatomical studies was developing and attracting attention.

From 1640 to approximately 1760 was a period during which the deceased could exercise control over the methods by which relatives and friends could influence funeral rites. The power to do this was, legally if not in actual practice, vested in the executors of the deceased. However, from 1680 onwards the profession of undertaker appeared, first in London, where population was concentrated at the highest level, then gradually spreading to other towns and cities. In rural areas there was insufficient business to support a full-time undertaker so the business became what it remained until the present day − a side-line for joiners and carpenters who supplied made-to-measure coffins, entirely made by hand, of oak or elm with highly finished and polished exteriors and lined with fabric. As time passed, undertaking became a specialized profession and undertakers were able to provide clients with a range of options from which to choose. They were also able to bring considerable pressure to bear so that it was the undertaker rather than the client who really called the tune.

Originally, executors were chiefly responsible for decisions made about funerals. Usually they were friends or neighbours of the deceased, as the cases to be studied will reveal. They also had the duty to obtain probate of the will and see that the wishes of the testator were carried out. In those cases where funeral directions were recorded in the will, the executors could ignore these if they so desired, for such requests are not legally enforceable but merely serve as an indication of the testator's wishes.

One aspect of funerals that has survived the traumas of the past and still exists is the practice of eating and drinking both before and after the funeral. In rural parishes, even today, the mourners are served with a glass of whisky (if the weather is cold) or a glass of wine and biscuits before leaving for the church or the crematorium. It is the secular rather than the religious aspect of the funeral that has led to the survival of this custom. The orthodox clergy at the time of the Reformation had little success in their eagerness to abolish ancient rituals, and the hard-line Puritan clergy even less. Once the burial office and the interment were concluded, the assembled mourners would return to the house of the deceased to take part in a 'drinking', which formed an essential part of the funeral rites.

The Restoration of the monarchy and the church in 1660, after the experience of the Cromwellian experiment, saw an ever-increasing emphasis being placed on the secular side of funerals. This was marked by the transfer of much of the ritual from the church to the residence of the deceased, which became the setting for a major part of the funeral rituals. Mourners began to spend more time at the home of the deceased than they spent in church. This change served to distinguish, somewhat forcefully, one funeral from another for both mourners and guests, since it emphasized the setting and individuality rather than the similarity between funerals of different persons in society. This encouraged both mourners and guests, but especially the latter, to make comparisons. Samuel Pepys, when he described the burial of his brother on 18 March

1664, gives an eyewitness account of the proceedings prior to setting out for the church.

> I dressed myself . . . and so to my brother's again: whither, though invited, as the custom is, at one or two o'clock, they come not till four or five. But at last they come, many more than I bid; and my reckoning that I bid one hundred and twenty, but I believe there was nearer one hundred and fifty. Their service was six biscuits apiece, and what they pleased of burnt claret . . . the men sitting by themselves in some rooms and the women by themselves in others, very close, but yet room cnough.[44]

The introduction of Naples biscuits after 1660 saw them become popular fare among the towns folk. Occasionally these were wrapped in paper and taken home. Later the wrappers were overprinted with a pattern, usually a coffin or some other symbol of mortality. In northern communities it remained the custom to bake funeral cakes, which were known as 'arval' bread, which is derived from the Scandinavian 'arval' or Celtic 'arwyl' meaning a funeral entertainment.[45]

After the Restoration, the gentry provided vast quantities of traditional refreshment at their funerals. George Fothergill, one of the Craven gentry, provided 30 pounds of biscuits for the funeral of Elizabeth Currer of Kildwick in 1697. Ten gallons of claret wine, four gallons of canary wine, twenty-four dozen biscuits and 2 pounds of 'little biscuits' were bought for a Halifax funeral in 1672. The Lister family of Shibden Hall in Halifax bought 4 pounds of biscuits from James Mellin and a 'gallon of red wine and half a gallon of white wine' for a funeral in 1749.[46] From the early years of the seventeenth century onwards, the provision of cakes and biscuits formed an important element at the funerals of the majority of folks in northern England, but rationing and war caused a decline to set in by 1918. However, funeral biscuits continued to be provided until the Second World War, when they disappeared as the result of food rationing and are now no longer readily available.

This custom of eating and drinking served a variety of purposes in the funeral ritual. On the one hand it enabled the social standing of the deceased and his wealth, or the lack of it, to be displayed to the community. The funeral feast is often referred to as an entertainment and so it often was, for it is quite clear from contemporary evidence that there was considerable enjoyment at this feasting.

Henry Prescott was one who took pleasure in attending a funeral feast after the burial and also before the funeral with the friends of the deceased. When Henry Prescott's sister, Mrs Partington, died he records the events of the evening she died:

> I am with my brother Partington on the sad occasion of my sister's Funeral. Dr Thane declines the funeral sermon. . . .
> In the Evening with my Lord, Messrs Clutterbuck, Maryon, Callis at Dr Thane's, wee are treated with 6 Bottles of good Claret, the conversation easy and ends after 9.

On 25 October the funeral of Mrs Partington took place in the evening when 'After the Funeral wee return to my Brother Partingtons where a company stays together past 9'.[47]

No doubt this ritual assisted in, to some extent, reducing the sorrow aroused by the funeral. No less a person than Richard Hooker defended this tradition.

> For the comfort of those whose minds are, through natural affection pensive in such cases, no man can justly mislike the custom which the Jews had to end their burials with funeral banquets.[48]

The intention behind this funeral ritual was to reunite all the surviving members of a family.

Funeral rites have a tradition that is firmly based on custom and was one that continued to flourish, especially in the north, until the present century, when the events of the Second World War hastened its demise.[49] These rites exercised a powerful healing effect which should not be underestimated, for the sharing of food, the presence of certain groups at funerals, the giving of gifts (be they in money, food, scarves, gloves or hatbands) all helped to reduce the consequences of death in a community.

It is clear from funeral accounts that more money and time were spent on the customary ritual than on the burial office itself. Available evidence indicates that these drinkings and feastings were more for the living than for the dead as in the end they lessened the impact of death and the problems that it posed for a community.

It should be asked how many mourners and guests attended a funeral. These numbers are very difficult to discover, though some probate accounts state figures such as 'about 100 people' or 'about 50 persons attended the corpse to the church' or 'being one hundred persons at the least' and 'there being 300 persons or thereabouts at the burial'.[50]

An examination of the probate accounts reveals that a not inconsiderable sum of money was expended upon food and drink at many funerals. Elizabeth Harrop, widow of Benjamin Harrop acting as her husband's sole executor, produced a total inventory amounting to £19.19s.8d. The entertainment provided consisted of:

Cheese	6s.0d.
Ale	11s.8d.
Meat	4s.0d.
Bread	2s.0d.[51]

This was a relatively small sum compared with the cost of the food provided for the funeral of Benjamin Glover of Wakefield, when the mourners and guests consumed sixteen dozen cakes with cheese, ale and spices, plus meat, at a cost of 44s.4d.[52]

When Margaret Earle, now Spencer (she having remarried), provided for her deceased husband's funeral, she contented herself with listing only ale, cakes, bread and sugar, which amounted to £2.15s.0d., and added at the end 'victuals according to custom', a typical phrase used in the West Riding of Yorkshire.[53]

In the case of John Justiss, master cutler of Sheffield, who died in 1733, his widow spent more money on biscuits than on ale but very generously provided 18s. worth of wine. Sheffield cutlers were noted for the copious quantities of ale they consumed to clear the dust from their throats. The dust from the grinding wheels caused lung diseases that resulted in the life expectancy of a cutler being short.[54] Indeed, Justiss's last illness had involved the employment of watchers to attend to his needs by night and day for six weeks.

Sometimes money was spent on the provision of pipes and tobacco for the mourners and guests. These were among the items of food and drink provided for the funeral of Timothy

Coles, vicar of Cockerham, in 1733 when, according to the accounts:

John Stuzaker for twelve dozen of Ale	12s.0d.
John Fox for crape, pipes, tobacco, sugar	99s.0d.
Widow Nixon for bread and the Arval	£2.12s.0d.[55]

Likewise, the executors of John Myerscough of Rawcliffe paid widow Bana some 18s.4d for ale, bread and tobacco.[56]

Those who were wealthy were able to provide lavish entertainment. A yeoman farmer of Whitby, who died in 1760, provided a dinner for the mourners and guests. The funeral party consumed 110 dozen penny loaves of bread, nine large hams, eight legs of veal, 20 stones of beef, 16 stones of mutton, 15 stones of Cheshire cheese and 20 gallons of ale, a truly magnificent funeral meal.[57] The executors of Ralph Colly of Handley spent 72s. on food and drink for some sixty mourners.[58] Likewise the funeral dinner provided at the funeral of Richard Ducket of Claughton, in Garstang parish, cost over £10.[59]

The provision made for the funeral of Elizabeth Seacombe, the widow of a prosperous Liverpool merchant, was on a grand scale. Ale and biscuits were provided for those who called at the time of her death. The room in which she was laid out before the funeral was illuminated by candles. It is clear that she died from dropsy, as the surgeon who tapped her body was paid 10s. Visitors to the house before the funeral were supplied with ale, and on the funeral day itself ale, meat and sack were provided in abundance, in addition to gloves and hatbands, which were supplied to all male mourners.[60]

The incompetence of some executors could create problems when it came to accounting for the expenses at the funeral, as happened at the funeral of Robert Arkwright of Newsham in Goosenargh parish. Arkwright had died from the effects of falling from a cart and the amount of money spent on the funeral was £8. John Arkwright, the executor, 'not being able to read or write cannot exactly remember what sums were paid out'.[61]

Many people provided for some form of charitable bequests to the poor, which were usually in the form of doles, or food, or a sum of money to be invested and the interest received to be applied to the relief of needy and poor persons. Ralph Colly made provision that £3 worth of bread should be bought from John Ashton and Joshua Welshman and given to the poor,[62] and the executors of Timothy Coles, vicar of Cockerham, distributed 24s. worth of bread to the poor.[63]

It is evident that many of these charitable bequests were made from a Christian belief that to feed the poor was one of the gifts of charity and would earn the donor some merit after death and at the judgment. In other cases it is clear that bequests were made in final bid for salvation, especially when there were serious omissions in their lives of negligence, fraud, deceit or other undesirable traits which they considered must be rectified in their wills and so ensure salvation.

6

THE SOCIAL SCENE

Before entering upon a detailed study of contested wills, it is essential that some reference should be made to the society of the era and its structure.

The period from 1660 onwards saw the expansion of the market town. Professor Everett in his study of the market town says that 'each played a vital role in the lives of several thousand husbandmen and labourers'.[1] Dr J.D. Marshall emphasizes that these towns were in nature and spirit urban entities, with facilities, currents of sentiment and ways of living that were very different from those prevailing in the strictly rural areas. The small town citizen lived in much closer intimacy with his fellows and town residents maintained their connections with those of their rural relatives who were still alive, whatever their social groups.[2]

The town, it must be remembered, had a hinterland which often extended beyond the economic scene. It was the town that provided the doctors, lawyers, schools, often large ones, and religious facilities. Many such as Chester, Manchester, Preston and Halifax became military garrisons after 1715 and 1745. A town was also a magnet for immigrants from the rural areas, since opportunities existed for women as domestic servants and for tradesmen who wished to expand their business as well as for professional people.

In the seventeenth century Cumbria and Westmorland were the two poorest counties in England. In 1657, Cumbria was taxed at £92.11s.4d. per month, which was the same as Exeter city, and Westmorland at £73.19s.6d., which was very low. By comparison, Essex and London were taxed at £3,000 and £4,000 respectively, but it must be remembered that the population in the north, considering the large acreage of land, was small.[3]

46

The Herald's Visitation of 1665 suggests that by this date Cockermouth was a very prosperous town in Cumbria whose wealth had accumulated through the wool trade. By 1660 Whitehaven, which in 1642 had but forty-five houses, was a market town. Under the leadership of the Lowther family it became a coal-mining centre and a seaport for trade with the American Colonies. By 1693, when the new chapel of St Nicholas was consecrated, the population had grown to 2,200. This example set by the Lowthers was adopted by the Curwen family in their town of Workington, which began to export coal by 1650. By 1724, Whitehaven had overtaken Cockermouth as the most prosperous town. Defoe in his tour said that 200 ships at one time sailed to Dublin with coal, and between 1739 and 1740 nearly 4 million pounds of tobacco were imported from Virginia. However, there was not a great deal of industrial development and the hinterland remained a rural one.[4]

By contrast, the Lancashire hundreds of West Derby and Salford were densely populated and contained the large towns of Manchester, Oldham, Rochdale and Wigan. Coal was being exploited and many men were operating a coal mine alongside agriculture.

In north Lancashire there were only two towns of any importance – Kirkham and Lancaster. The rest of the region was agricultural and composed of a number of small parishes, with a very scattered population between the Ribble and the Wyre.[5]

The borderland between Yorkshire and Lancashire was an area of wild, uncultivated moorland country, supporting a thinly spread population. Few farms exceeded 600 acres and many were less than 200, with an average acreage per farm of 20–50. Lancashire agriculture in the eighteenth century was progressive. Small enclosures of land were taking place on a large scale and experiments were being conducted on enclosed wasteland.[6]

In the West Riding of Yorkshire the towns of Leeds, Halifax, Bradford and Huddersfield were expanding and a prosperous dual economy in agriculture and textiles was becoming established. Likewise, an expanding market in South Yorkshire at Doncaster was serving the needs of the growing hinterland.[7]

Gloucestershire was another county where industry and farming were expanding. Cotswold wool formed the basic prosperity of several towns and the proximity to Bristol provided Gloucester with an outlet to the sea. Lancashire, Yorkshire and Gloucester compared well with Cumbria and Westmorland, which were backward and very conservative. On the other hand, the towns of Whitehaven and Workington, with their shipping trade, were far more important than Liverpool, Hull and Bristol put together.

After 1660, agricultural prices stagnated, and this was aggravated by war taxation (especially after 1688) to finance the long war against the ambitions of Louis XIV. Despite this economic pressure, which squeezed many out into poverty, inventories from Cumbria and Westmorland show signs of rising living standards amongst the yeomen and tenant farmers. The inventories attached to wills record in detail all the items of a deceased person's worldy possessions, such as farming gear and household goods (including utensils), which provide evidence of the deceased's financial situation. Animals such as sheep, cattle, horses and pigs were found on all farms. By 1660 the furniture found in the farmhouse begins to reveal an increasing prosperity: pillows, sheets and blankets were in general use. However, since bedding and bedsteads were frequently lumped together in the inventory, precise numbers are difficult to obtain.

The majority of families, with the exception of the very poor, had two or three beds and about the same number of tables and chairs. In addition, there could be an ark, or a cupboard or a chest, and sometimes all three items. Pewter and brass were in general use and could form grounds for a dispute. Only the gentry and prosperous yeomen had silver. Brass candlesticks and brass pans were by no means uncommon and several arguments about the ownership of such items appear in contested wills. Even looking or seeing glasses were not rare.[8]

Wearing apparel appears to have been in the range of £1 to £3 in value, though better-off folk could reach £10. Likewise, funeral expenses could range from £5 to £20 or £30.

Investigating contested wills has allowed an intimate knowledge of the attitudes, preoccupations and way of life of people from the middle to the bottom (or close to it) of the social scale.

It is clear that family relationships were more loving and caring than some recent historians have claimed. Lawrence

Stone, describing human nature at the beginning of the seventeenth century, gives a depressing account of human relationships. He states that there was a 'lack of warmth and tolerance' and that personal relationships were cold and hostile.[9] Edward Shorter referred to this period as the 'Bad Old Days' of European family history.[10]

Allowance must be made for the unpredictable variety of family life. In the world of the late seventeenth and early eighteenth century life was more uncertain than it is at the present day, for hygiene was little known, health care very limited and poverty far more immediate, as can be found in the diaries of Oliver Heywood, John Hobson of Dodworth and Ralph Thoresby of Leeds.[11] It is impossible to pursue a study of this nature with firmly set ideas of what should have happened.

The extended family was not particularly powerful in early modern England, so ties between the nuclear family and the wider circle of relatives were in all probability weak. The important occasions of family life were marked by the three important stages in life, those of baptism, marriage and burial, which drew the wider circle of relatives together. On the whole it is clear from the evidence contained in the wills under discussion that people resorted to their relatives or intimate friends when advice was needed rather than material help. The diary of Henry Prescott illustrates this point in the precise manner in which he records his contacts with a wider network of relatives in Wigan and North Wales. There are also many clues as to the way in which individuals should behave towards their relatives.[12] Certainly, feelings and a sense of family could extend outside the nuclear household. The families involved in this study, as also families in general, can best be studied in the context of connected institutions where service, friendship and neighbourhood are most important.

The amount of symbolic capital that lay in a good name or reputation is an aspect that would have been considered to be of vital importance. The term 'credit', which occurs so frequently in any contested case that arose in this period, was not merely an economic term, but was used in the sense of having a reputation or standing in the community. Privacy was by no means a familiar concept, for parishioners were always to be seen and their conduct observed and assessed by their neighbours, supplemented by their neighbours' comments and gossip. In reality the concept of neighbourliness was connected with the Christian ideal 'living in love and charity with all men'[13] and formed a working model on which to found one's behaviour.

Indeed, there is evidence in the libel and depositions of witnesses, where a will is contested in the court, pointing to the presence of strong ideals of mutual obligation, of friendship and of neighbourliness, and a very clearly defined notion of proper human conduct. For instance, Anne Richardson, a widow from Wistow, left a cow in her will to another widow in the same parish in 1658 for 'her care and paines taken about me in my sickness'. And Matthew Newcome, a tailor of Riccall left a woman 3s, 'for her diligence and care she has taken with me and hath been ready to doe earants and run for mee here and there'.[14]

The many references in contested wills to the 'deceased's friends' pose the question: who were one's friends? By the eighteenth century they were, in the first rank, one's relatives. Mrs Malaprop in *The Rivals* exhorted her niece to 'take a husband of your friends' choosing', meaning of course her aunt. William Wright in *The Complete Tradesman* argued the apprentice's right to the advantages 'for which he had served his time and for which his friends gave a considerable sum of money with him'.[15] Secondly, friends could be members of one's household such as the children's tutor, and thirdly they could be one's tenants and villagers.

Patronage was important because it was a 'vertical friendship', a durable two-way relationship between patrons and clients which permeated the whole of society. It was such an integral part of life that the only word they could find for it was 'friendship'. It was the module on which the social structure was built, for the vertical links united the interest pyramids which embraced every level of society from the great landowners and merchants, down to mere labourers.

Outside the home and family larger units of organization played a greater part in shaping and controlling the life of an individual than they do at the present time. The size of the unit varied widely – from the very small villages and hamlets in the rural deaneries of Copeland and Kendal, many with fewer than 100 inhabitants, to a large city such as York or London. It was in these varied settlements that people were born, grew up, met their future partners, got married, had children, learnt trades associated with their fellow humans and in time died.

A new appraisal of the rural scene has to be made in the light of information presented in the large number of local histories that are produced. One belief that can now be discarded is that the pre-industrial village had a stable population that experienced low geographical mobility. Our rural ancestors did not live like cabbages, rooted in one place, neither was the pre-industrial village a static community of 'sociological and historical received wisdom'.[16] Certainly the village community was a 'face-to-face' society, but the faces were constantly changing.

During the sixteenth and seventeenth centuries, as agriculture became capitalized, so there took place some polarization in village society. There was a layer of comfortable yeomen farmers and master craftsmen on one side, and a large body of labouring poor on the other. The definition of social inferiors during these two centuries is difficult. There was no term that corresponded to the modern 'working class'. Both 'yeoman' and 'husbandman' were loose descriptions which encompassed men with vastly different levels of wealth. The term 'labourer' was used to define anyone from a skilled farm worker, with a smallholding of a few acres of land, some livestock and pasture rights, to a mere 'daytailer', one who worked for wages and was paid by the day.

The gaps opening up in so many villages make it unwise to discuss the village community in simplistic terms. By 1750 it is better to speak of two cultures, one of prosperous farmers and the other of labouring poor. The nineteenth-century supposition that idyllic social relationships had existed in rural areas before the Industrial Revolution is a complete myth – one that gave rise to the 'Merrie England' that has become part of popular thinking. On the other hand, any pessimistic view of village relationships is inaccurate and oversimplified.

Part II

THE
VULTURES DESCEND

7

FRAUDULENT EXECUTORS

In the same manner as vultures gather in the desert waiting for the death of a sick animal, so in society many people behave like vultures when the time arrives for reading the will. Once the funeral rites were concluded and the funeral dinner over, then the disposal of the effects of the deceased person became of prime importance. One feature that a study of contested wills reveals is family relationships, which in the majority of cases emphasize the sins of envy, hatred, pride, greed and what the Prayer Book litany terms 'blindness of heart and all uncharitableness'. Executors as well as relatives could be devious and therefore somewhat difficult to deal with in such cases.

Examples of this type of person are to be found in a large number of contested wills. The will of Elizabeth Harrison of Neatley in Garstang parish, who died in 1719, illustrates the problems that can arise when one of the family is appointed executor. In this case, William Jackson, son-in-law of Elizabeth Harrison deceased, was accused of fraudulent conversion of the deceased's goods on the grounds that he did 'temarariously, rashly & of your own head & without any lawfull authority seized upon and possess yourself of several of the goods & Chattels of the deceased & particularly the goods . . . mentioned and converted the same to your own use'.[1] Legally, all persons who presumed to interfere with the administration of the goods of any deceased persons, without obtaining probate, were liable to be prosecuted and punished.

William Jackson said he had provided all things for Elizabeth Harrison during her last sickness and for the whole of the time when she lived with the Jacksons, where eventually she died. Thomasine Harrison, granddaughter of Elizabeth

Harrison deceased, a young woman of 28 years of age, said that she was informed by Elizabeth Jackson, wife of William, that 'there was a Bedd and Bedding, Bolsters and Sheets', which were shown to her in Jackson's house shortly after the death of Elizabeth Harrison. Elizabeth Jackson said that the bed was 'the old woman's' and went on to state that Elizabeth Harrison 'always lay in the said Bedd wherever she went and dy'd in it'. Clearly Elizabeth Harrison carried her bed with her wherever she went to lodge.

The Jacobite rebellion of 1715 had been centred on the area round Garstang and Preston. In order to keep the area under surveillance, the government maintained a garrison in the district. In accordance with the practice at this time, soldiers were often billeted on householders and one of these was Elizabeth Jackson. A few days after the death of Elizabeth Harrison, Elizabeth Jackson came to remove the bed and bedding to provide sleeping accommodation for the soldiers now billeted in her house.

The day following the funeral, Elizabeth Jackson produced, in the presence of Thomasine Harrison and other witnesses, 3s. 6³/4d., which she had found in the 'old woman's pocket', meaning her mother's. Further, William Jackson, who disliked Thomasine Harrison's mother, Elizabeth, who was in very poor circumstances and receiving poor relief from the parish, said that if she continued to encourage Thomasine to make trouble he would see that 'she should have no relief out of the town'. The morning after the funeral Elizabeth Harrison came and demanded her mother's goods and effects, which William Jackson refused to surrender. The goods in question were but few and amounted to these items:

1 feather bed, bedstead and bolster, pillow and blankets, sheets and a rug.   £1.0s.0d.

Her purse and apparell viz; 2 Mantuas, 5 petticoats, 2 shifts, 10 caps, a hat and other linen and wearing Cloaths   17s.6d.

Item; other implements in her possession when she died   £1.10s.0d.

Goods and money in the hands of William Jackson at the time of her death   £120.0s.0d.

This sum does not justify the claim that she was a poor woman.

Rather the Jacksons were greedy, as was confirmed by Grace Wilkinson, the wife of George Wilkinson, a yeoman, who stated that she knew the deceased very well but she was amazed to learn that she died possessed of both money and goods, for Elizabeth Jackson always maintained that there was only a 'certain old Bedd which was the old woman's Bedd'. In the opinion of this witness that bed was worth no more than 5s. and the 3s. 6d. found in the deceased's pocket was money she earned by spinning wool.

Isabel Clarkson, a widow from Neatly aged 68 years, was one of those women found in every village whose profession it was to prepare the body of a deceased person for burial. In this case she had provided her services for Elizabeth Harrison. However, instead of paying Isabel the customary fee for her services, Elizabeth Jackson had given her the deceased's clothes. These consisted of 'a pair of bodys, a coif and a pair of stockings which the old woman had worn in her lifetime'. Isabel was most displeased at being given a bundle of second-hand clothing as payment, so she revealed information about the existence of an annuity.

It appeared that a contract had been agreed between William Jackson and Elizabeth Harrison, some four years before her death, that the former would pay to the latter the sum of £3.10s.0d. annually during her lifetime towards her mainte-nance. Isabel was convinced that this agreed sum had never been paid in full and that there were considerable arrears as yet unpaid. Then she added that the deceased had very often complained that Jackson never paid the money at the places where she was boarded, and that the value of the goods given to her in lieu of the money that she should have received for her services at the funeral was not above 6d.

Ellen Sidgreave, the wife of the joiner Thomas Sidgreave, stated that she had no idea that Elizabeth Harrison had any money or goods at the time of her death. However, Elizabeth Jackson had sold her a petticoat for 2s., which she said had belonged to 'the old woman', meaning her mother.

Another relative was William Killerach, linen weaver, who said he knew the deceased very well indeed for she was his wife's grandmother. He had no idea that she possessed either money or goods or even chattels, with the exception of a feather bed and 'some few wearing apparell which were removed from his house by one of William Jackson's servants, but he had no knowledge as to their present whereabouts'.

The judge agreed that Jackson had quite illegally administered the effects of Elizabeth Harrison's estate and he was condemned in costs and the sentence of greater excommunication was passed upon him.[2]

Legacies, debts and embezzlement were the basis of the cause brought by John Wilson, nephew of William Herd, against Richard Shuttleworth and James Brindley of Alston in Ribbleton, executors of William Herd deceased. John Wilson alleged that Herd had bequeathed £10 each to his two nephews Thomas and James Wilson and the same sum to his nephew John Wilson and also to his niece Elizabeth Wilson, which legacies were to be paid 'Twelve months after my decease'.

Richard Staningstreet, yeoman of Goosenargh, stated that on 29 April 1727, shortly after the death of Herd, John Wilson, the plaintiff in the cause, was indebted to Staningstreet in the sum of £6.15s.10d. for wool delivered to him for spinning into yarn, there being a strong domestic textile industry in the area. Staningstreet claimed that Wilson had embezzled the wool and made no attempt to make satisfaction for the debt. Hence, Staningstreet had no other option than to cite Wilson to appear before the magistrates at Quarter Sessions, when the court ordered Wilson to make immediate satisfaction for the wool and draw a bill on the executors asking them to meet the debt from his legacy. Wilson objected to the order and stated that he hoped to clear the debt from his own resources before the legacy bequeathed to him by Herd was due to be paid and laying the blame on the executors as totally incompetent.

The executors stated that on 29 April 1727 Wilson had been arrested on the petition of Staningstreet for non-payment of debt and was taken into custody. At this point Wilson wrote to Shuttleworth asking him to pay the debt out of the legacy, which he accordingly did. Shuttleworth offered the balance of £3.4s.2d. to Wilson, but as it was not in coin Wilson refused to accept it.

Appearing before Mr Justice Chadock at the Mitre Inn in Preston, Shuttleworth immediately handed to Staningstreet a draft for £6.15s.10d. payable in eight months, but after the months had passed the draft had not been met. The legacy was due to be paid on 30 April last, but Shuttleworth had made no further approach and Wilson believed he 'was neither ready nor willing' to clear the debt. Sentence was then given in favour of Wilson.[3]

Bonds and obligations could be a source of friction in the settlement of an estate. In 1729 Thomas Award of Goosenargh had appointed Henry Bryers and Alexander Bleasdale of Chipping to be his executors. Shortly after Award's death they were approached by Jeremiah Waring concerning a debt of £24 under a bond and obligation, the sum claimed being the penal amount. The terms of the obligation were to pay the sum of £12 with interest. It appeared that the bond had been drawn up several years before the death of Award and the agreed sum with interest remained as yet unpaid.

The executors seem to have been somewhat devious in this matter, since they promised to pay the debt but in reality all that was handed over was the 12s. interest due on the bond and not the capital sum. The executors admitted that they had sufficient resources to clear the bond although they had promised to do so by the previous 15 October under a court order obtained by Waring. Waring then expressed his complete lack of confidence in them, for 'they did trifle and by their false and fictitious allegations' delayed the payment of the debt. In an attempt to dodge the issue, the executors claimed that the funeral charges and administration expenses would be the first charge on the estate and the debts would be cleared, from the proceeds of the sale of the deceased's effects, when sufficient funds were raised to clear the debt.[4]

An executor could be placed in a difficult situation when obliged to place the deceased's property in full repair, a matter which some attempted to ignore. In 1710, Ellen Ryley, the daughter of George Clayton of Wadley Street, Fulwood, accused William Clayton, the executor, that he had neglected his responsibility to repair the property. In fact the property had not been maintained by George Clayton and was in serious decay. When challenged by Ellen Ryley concerning his negligence, William replied that 'he had not yet repaired the cottage nor set any term to it, being so precarious and the charges of reparation being so great, he would reap no benefit from it'. In fact, William openly admitted that he would lose heavily if he did repair it.

Being challenged concerning omissions from the inventory, he agreed that he had forgotten to include the value of two mares and 20s., being the cost of feeding them, neither had he paid Ellen Ryley her costs of £10. The judge found him guilty of misrepresentation and sentenced him to pay costs.[5]

Margaret Anyon, a widow in St Oswald's parish in Chester, kept an alehouse and when she died her will was contested by Alice Anyon, the wife of John Anyon, on the grounds that the executors, Alderman William Street and John Taylor, had used undue influence on the testatrix, who, she claimed, was incapable of making a will. In the course of his evidence Alderman Street said that Margaret Anyon, 'being sick', sent for him. When he arrived and entered the room in which she lay, Margaret ordered the door to be closed and asked him to draw up her will. In his defence he claimed that 'he has not interferred in the estate, nor doth he hope for any advantage from the said will having renounced all his rights and advantages'.

One witness in the cause was Margaret Locker of Northgate Street, Chester, who was a poor widow of 72 years of age. Being poor she was open to suspicion that she would be ready to accept bribes and succumb to undue influence. Her evidence was admitted on the grounds that she had attended Margaret Anyon in her last illness. She pointed out that, on the Thursday or Friday before her death, Alderman Street and John Taylor came with Mrs Taylor into the room where Margaret lay. After some conversation, a table was brought to the bedside with pen, ink and papers. As Alderman Street commenced to write, she and Mrs Taylor left the room.

When the will was completed, Godfrey Malbon and Samuel Docker, the tapster of the house, were summoned into the room and asked to witness the will by setting their marks to it. Alderman Street then enquired if Margaret had said all that she wished to say or if there were items in the will she wished to change. Having agreed that everything was in order, Alderman Street left, and Margaret Anyon died the following Monday morning.

Margaret Locker admitted that she was a poor widow, but she had had a good house in Northgate Street which was burned in the siege of Chester during the Civil War. She had since moved to a small house which she could occupy for life. She admitted that she 'took great pains for her living' and hoped that she had sufficient money to pay for all she owed. Another widow, Alice

Briscoe, also confirmed that she worked for her living and did not owe more than 8s.

Godfrey Malbon, a grocer aged 30 years, said he was clerk to Margaret at the time of her death, keeping and writing up her accounts and attending to her business affairs, a task he had undertaken for the past nine years. Working in the house on Friday 30 May last, he was called by one of the maids to come to the room, where he found Alderman Street, John Taylor and his wife with Margaret Anyon, with the will laid out before her. When the deceased sat up in bed, Alderman Street explained to her what it was and handed her a pen. The deceased said she was too weak to hold it or to sign her name, so Alderman Street told her to make her mark. This agreed, the two witnesses made their marks.

On the Monday morning, a few hours after her death, John Taylor called and said that, as Malbon understood her affairs better than he did, he wished him to continue in his old employment and to have the same allowance or a better one than previously, so he had continued in his former employment. He confirmed that the greatest part of the deceased's estate was in household goods not yet valued, also that there were some debts owing to her that were good and some that were bad. Further, there was not more than £10 in money in the house.

However, Samuel Dockrey, the tapster aged 50 years, who was a servant to Margaret Anyon for many years, like others before and since had hopes of an inheritance only to be disappointed. Having witnessed the will alongside Malbon, he was amazed to discover that nothing had been left to him in the will. His comment was that in his opinion Margaret Anyon was totally incapable of making a will, for she would have left some legacies to her servants 'as she had done in a former will'. In the end, Alice Anyon lost her cause and had to pay all the costs and expenses that arose for attempting to frustrate the duties of the executors.[6]

Matters could be very difficult indeed for a widow when confronted by men who claimed to be her husband's executors. The day following the funeral of William Curwen, three men came to the house and persuaded Isabel Curwen, the widow, to give them power and authority to sell and dispose of those goods and chattels she wished to sell. The men were John Jackson, James Good and William Simpson, the curate of Lightburn in Ulverston. The three 'executors' set about their task with crafty designs. They claimed that they would be able to undertake the disposal more advantageously than Isabel could do, 'Not for money or gain but out of the love and respect they had for her'.

Naturally, the death of her husband caused Isabel Curwen to be 'stricken with grief' and therefore in a state of mind in which people could impose on her. She was unable to resist the pressure 'from fair speeches, false Insinuations and entertaining offers and promises given to her by the pretended executors'. She yielded to their blandishments and signed a deed of attorney appointing them to exercise a legal authority to administer the estate. Later Isabel said that she was totally unaware of the contents of the document she had signed but, by devious methods, the three executors managed to get possession of the will and take it into their custody.

It appeared that, some twelve or fifteen years earlier, William Curwen, as the result of a violent fright from a beast or other means, became 'Craz'd, distracted and a Melancholy man and void of his understanding, frequently threatened to be his own Executioner'. At the same time he would tear the clothes from his body or else quite literally cover himself with clothes and 'doing other raving mad and extravagent actions'. He had a phobia against his friends and relatives so that when they called he would either run behind the door or crawl under the table, shouting out in terror, 'Shut, shut'. At table he both ate and drank 'gluttonously like a Beast'. At other times, he would 'grease the outside of his Throat, Breast and Stomach' in the belief that by doing so his appetite would be enormously increased.

As William was totally incapable of managing his own affairs, his brother, Emmanuel Curwen, undertook this responsibility until he died. Then, by force of circumstance, Isabel was compelled to obtain the assistance of friends and neighbours, especially James Nelson, to act for her husband 'in buying, selling and settling of lands'. During the hearing of the cause in court, it was revealed that Curwen had never had the will in contest read to him, neither had William Simpson nor any other witness. It was believed that Simpson deluded Curwen into dictating his will to him, totally contradicting a previous will because Simpson was expecting that he would obtain the residue of the estate.

Originally, Curwen had appointed his close friend James Nelson as sole executor, a decision that outraged Simpson so much that 'he chid Curwen in a very churlish manner', which terrified him to such an extent that he was forced to submit, contrary to his inclinations, to make Nelson a legatee only. When he instructed Simpson to include in the will a legacy of £50 to Nelson, Simpson was furious and, 'with a great deal of harsh language', compelled Curwen to reduce this to £40, but in the pretended will this had again been reduced to a mere £5. A legacy of 10s. a year to Edward Gryson was amended to one single payment, as were two further legacies of 10s. a year to Esther Ashburner and Elizabeth Borwick.

Furthermore, it had been Curwen's intention that his wife Isabel should receive one half of her legacy for the duration of her natural life, even if she entered upon a second marriage, but in that case payment of the second half would cease when the marriage took place. Simpson would have none of it, and changed the will by inserting a clause that ensured that she would have to remain a widow for the remainder of her life.

Further evidence revealed that Simpson had ignored the deceased's wishes as he had omitted several legacies to friends and neighbours, especially 'a pair of Bedstocks' which were to be given to Leonard Fell. When the pretended will was produced for probate, Simpson was openly accused by Isabel Curwen, plaintiff, of 'treachery and unfair and deceitful practice' in a variety of forms and alienating the directions and true intentions of William Curwen.

The plaintiff added further information by stating that Simpson had used 'unfair arts and strattagems' to get Curwen to sign his will, 'by dragging him and forcing him out of his Bedchamber'. Naturally, Curwen was most unwilling to sign the will but the curate Simpson by 'an imperious and rude manner compelled him to sign'. Finally, having refused Curwen's request for the will to be left with him for further consideration, Simpson left, taking the will with him.

At this point, Simpson realised that his case was beginning to collapse. He became afraid and 'he fell into utter confusion'. Simpson made one last effort to get himself out of the mess. He approached Nelson, who 'had taxed him with foul dealings', asking him to keep quiet on all these matters, and in return he would reward him very generously at Nelson's own price, if only he would agree to the proposals in the will.

When it was examined, the date on the original will proved to be prior to the deterioration of Curwen's mind, a matter that was confirmed by the majority of his neighbours who had known him. It was also revealed that, contrary to custom, the pretended executors were neither relatives nor close friends of the deceased 'who did any act of friendship' – an important fact in the appointment of executors at this period. Neither John Jackson nor James Good knew they were executors until they were nominated by Simpson, or that they were to share with him in the residue of the estate.

In the light of all this evidence, Isabel Curwen requested that the will produced for probate should be declared null and void, with the pretended executors sentenced to pay full costs in the cause. Her request for right and justice to be done was accepted and she was legally appointed as administratrix of the estate; Simpson and his cronies had to pay full costs.[7]

A nephew who expected to inherit his uncle's estate and also act as executor received similar treatment to that given to Simpson. Edward Sherwen of Whitehaven had been a 'master marriner' who had charge of a ship trading to America. He died a bachelor in 1732. He had a nephew Thomas Benn, who stated that during his lifetime his uncle Edward Sherwen had promised to leave him his private pew in Holy Trinity Church, Whitehaven, and his silver punch bowl, but when the will was read Benn discovered that these items had been bequeathed to Joseph Barrow. Benn, feeling wronged, commenced a cause in court to prove that his uncle was not in his right mind when he made his will.

Richard Brownrigg, husbandman of Gosforth, aged 50, stated that in January 1732 he was in the company of Edward Sherwin in Thomas Benn's house, having some business to transact with Benn. When he entered the house he found Sherwin 'sitting by the kitchen fire'. Sherwin then engaged Brownrigg in conversation, replying readily to Sherwin's questions about his relatives in Gosforth and news of any events there. As far as Brownrigg was concerned, Sherwin appeared to be sensible, rational and capable of making his own will, but in the February of 1732 Sherwin was dead.

William Gilpin, a merchant friend of Sherwin, said he had known him for many years but more especially towards the end of his life. In the summer of 1731 Sherwin came to him to receive payment of money due to him, and also again on 23 December. On both occasions he was sensible and gave a receipt for the money but, apart from that, there were no further dealings between them. However, there were reports in Whitehaven about Sherwin's visits to alehouses.

Eleanor Branthwaite, a spinster aged 19 years and a former servant to Mrs Ann Bell, who kept an alehouse, provided further details. She knew Sherwin very well for he was a regular customer, as sensible as any who went to that house and quite capable of managing his own affairs. When questioned further she replied that she had never heard Sherwin express 'any Dislike or Aversion to Mr Thomas Benn his nephew', but when he was drunk, which was frequently the case, 'he would not go home without assistance'. Indeed, during her time as Mrs Bell's servant she often conducted Sherwin home when he was drunk. On those occasions when he stayed late at Mrs Bell's, Henry Townson, servant to Mr Barrow, took him to his lodging.

Peter Howe, a Whitehaven merchant, first met Sherwin in 1714 when he was a ship's master. In 1715 he went into partnership with Sherwin and together they made two foreign voyages. As a result of this enterprise Sherwin cleared £700. When Sherwin retired in 1730 he had made a fortune of £1400. Howe then acquired a rope works and in the summer of 1731, while working in the factory, Sherwin came to him (about six months before he died) and Howe reminded him of a debt that was ten years old. When Howe mentioned this, Sherwin recalled the occasion and promised to leave him 'ten pounds to buy a Mourning suit for his funeral'. There followed no further contact with the deceased except when they met in the street.

When Howe was questioned about Sherwin's addiction to drink, he remarked that he had known him for seventeen years but had never been in his company in an alehouse, except once or twice. However, he had overheard in conversation that Sherwin 'very much frequented Alehouses and was very often overseen in Liquor within two years before his death'. During this period Sherwin began to be seen less frequently in the company of his old acquaintances but instead began to frequent the company more of 'Persons of inferior rank but for what reason he does not know'. Indeed, towards the close of his life he became more addicted to drink than he used to be and, like so many others then as now, became very abusive when drunk.

Joshua Webster probably indicates the reason why Sherwin changed his mind, for he had heard that sometime before 19 November 1731 Thomas Benn had refused to give Sherwin any pocket money when he asked for it. During the first week in January 1731/2 Webster was invited to dinner at Mrs Richardson's inn in Whitehaven, but not arriving until dinner was ended he found Sherwin in the company of Ben Tideman, William Barley and many others. He was invited to sit down with the company, and Sherwin expressed his opinion that he 'should not live long'. Whereupon, Barley asked him to leave him his clothes, to which he replied that if 'he did this then Thomas Benn would cheat you of them. He swore that he would set Mr Barrow on him for there was not one that could match Tom Benns but Mr Barrow.' Having known Sherwin for twenty years, Webster assumed that he intended to make Barrow his executor and not Thomas Benn.

Webster admitted that he often drank a pot of ale with Sherwin because Sherwin enjoyed conversing on the news of the town. He then gave a small picture of Sherwin's character, 'being a Gentleman of Merry Facetous Temper and very Inquisitive about all Occurences that might happen from time to time'.

Ben Tideman, another merchant acquaintance, revealed that he had known Sherwin for twenty years and once heard him say that he had only £50 to start up in business, but by sheer hard work rose to become a ship's master. For many years Sherwin was involved in merchant shipping in which he made a fortune. He often complained about the behaviour of his nephew Thomas Benn, who refused 'to pay him what was due to him', so Sherwin came to dislike Benn and Tideman understood from conversation that Barrow was to be his executor.

On 7 June 1726 an indenture had been made between Sherwin and Thomas Benn that, in return for £30 in cash, Sherwin would acquit Benn from a Bond to pay him a sum of money each year for the rest of his natural life. He also sold to Benn 'all his messuage standing on the south west of Lowther Street and continuing in the front corner of Scotch Street south east for eleven yards and backwards from the front thirty yards and also the garden adjoining being thirty yards by forty'.[8] His pew in Whitehaven church was also sold to Benn.

A friend of long standing, one William Barley, also a mariner, came to see him when he came to visit Whitehaven from Cockermouth in January 1731/2. At this meeting Sherwin said that 'he thought he would not live long and died within a fortnight' of this meeting. His conversation was always on sea-faring matters but he drank too heavily and his old merchant friends who usually drank with him, Mr Stow, Mr Coats and Will Parish, were now all of them dead.

The root cause of the trouble between uncle and nephew was that Benn claimed his uncle had promised to leave him his silver punch bowl and his pew in Holy Trinity Church, Whitehaven, which was mentioned in a will of 2 September 1708. Benn also said there had been a deed of bargain and sale concerning the pew and the punch bowl.

Between this date and 1731 relationships between Sherwin and Benn had broken down, so, on 19 November 1731, Sherwin made a second will in which he wrote; 'I give and bequeath to Joseph Barrow of Whitehaven, Gentleman all that my Seat or Pew in the new Chapel of Whitehaven aforesaid together with my Silver Punch Bowl'. Fearful of losing this valuable property, Benn contested the second will on the grounds that his uncle's sanity had deteriorated when he made this second will. However, Benn was unable to provide proof that a deed of bargain and sale had taken place. Benn never appeared in court so the will of 1708 was declared to be null and void on 22 May 1734 and Joseph Barrow was declared to be the sole executor.[9]

A deliberate attempt at fraud is found in the dispute between Ann Richardson, the widow of William Taylor, who had died intestate at Border Rig, and Robert Askew of Broughton and John Denny also of Border Rig, being the supposed executors of the deceased. Administration of the estate was granted to Ann Richardson, now the wife of Joseph Richardson (she had remarried shortly after her first husband's death). At the time when John Taylor drew up his father's will, the heir to the estate was an unborn infant in his mother's womb. In his will dated 6 January 1715 Taylor had said:

> It is my will and mind that the Infant in the mother's Belly if it pleaseth the Lord, it be born alive, shall have the sum of sixty pounds and if it be a Living or Dead Child, or afterwards dye, then the said sixty pounds is to go to my son John his heirs or assigns. I appoint Charles Satterthwaite, Robert Askew and William Jackson my servant to be my supervisors. The rest of my goods I give unto my beloved wife Ann Taylor whom I hereby Constitute and Appoint to be my sole executrix.

Ann Richardson took upon herself the duty to prove the will and the administration of it, declaring that the 'Infant in the Mother's Belly was William Taylor then in her womb'. The child was born alive but, being a sickly child, only lived to the age of 13 years.

The legacy of £60 should, under the terms of the will, have passed to his son John Taylor, the son of Ann Taylor, for he was the heir at law and already in possession of a considerable estate from his father.

The task of administering an estate like John Taylor's was too great a responsibility for men of the calibre of Askew and Denny. They were convinced that they could alienate a considerable portion of the estate into their own pockets because it would be easy to manipulate Ann Richardson. The two executors immediately possessed themselves of all 'books, bonds, bills, mortgages and other securities', refusing to render any account but simply converting the assets to their own use and so defrauding the lawful heirs.

Ann was too quick for them: she went to court and obtained an order to compel the executors to render an account to her so that she could produce a correct inventory for probate. Both Askew and Denny remained obstinate and openly refused to deliver any bonds, bills and mortgages or to produce any account of them, for they had converted the same to their own use.

At the court hearing, the judge stated that Askew and Denny should have handed over all the interest on 'bond, bill or mortgage', to either Ann or Joseph Richardson for the proper maintenance and education of William Taylor during his lifetime and to cover the cost of the funeral when the boy died. The judge pronounced that, for their deceitful actions, both men were sentenced to pay full costs and at the same time suffer the sentence of greater excommunication.[10]

Cases of this nature are not confined to one area of the country; similar instances can be found elsewhere. In 1725, William Rodwell, of the Levels in Thorne parish near Doncaster, died and his brother Thomas Rodwell, vicar of Arksey, acted as executor, only to be challenged by John Simpson on the following grounds: on the death of his brother, Thomas Rodwell had gone to court and exhibited a will dated 8 March 1720, so obtaining letters of administration on 8 October 1727 giving him authority to wind up the estate of his dead brother. Simpson claimed that, in the will exhibited in court, Phebe Rodwell, William's wife, was named as the sole executrix, but she had since died. On 2 April 1725, William made a second will which John Simpson knew existed. Simpson claimed that Thomas Rodwell had kept this will hidden, never informing him of its existence, so that he had obtained letters of administration on the first will.

Thomas Rodwell had no alternative but to produce the second will in court, although he had already taken possession of his brother's goods and effects.[11] The judge ordered that the goods and effects removed by Thomas Rodwell should be handed over to Simpson, who was granted letters of administration.

George Bateman found himself at variance with his mother-in-law, Elizabeth Noble, concerning the will of John Noble, tanner, of Fenwick in Campsall. John had appointed his wife Elizabeth as his executrix. However, she found herself being challenged on the grounds that she had omitted many items of goods, chattels and debts from the inventory, while an additional number were undervalued. The debts omitted were the following:

Lee Hartley of Pontefract	£30	on bond
Huan Duffield of Sherburn	£5	on bond
James Smith of Asselby	£10	
James Wordsworth of Asselby	£9	

Under the terms of the will, Elizabeth Noble was given the authority to sell any wood from the deceased's estate or grounds to the value of £30 to enable his debts to be paid and to provide for the children's portions under the custom of York. Elizabeth had allowed her son Thomas £40 for the leather in John Noble's tanpits over and above the money his father had given to him during his lifetime; not one of these items appeared in the inventory. Since the debts John Noble owed at the time of his death amounted to less than £6 no increase should be granted to the amount of money Elizabeth required. Further, the lands devised to Thomas and Nathaniel, his second son, together with the leather given to Thomas and £40 to Nathaniel, ought to be in satisfaction of their child's part with nothing to Elizabeth.

According to George Bateman, John Noble had left his daughter, Elizabeth, the late wife of George Batemen, £150 to be paid in two portions, one of £100 at the present time and a further £50 when her mother died. George also believed that the three executors – John Bateman of Snaith, Thomas Bradshaw of Hemsworth and Elizabeth Noble – had only entered bond for £100 for administering the estate. In his opinion it was quite within the bounds of probability that the three executors could become insolvent before Elizabeth Noble died and that, which was far more important, George Bateman might lose the £50 which was his late wife's portion.

In his evidence, George Bateman claimed that the value of John Noble's goods and chattels was far in excess of the £120 stated and that several items that ought to have been included in the inventory were not. While he believed that Elizabeth had paid the funeral expenses, the cost of valuing the goods, and her travelling expenses to York for probate and the fees due, yet he was not convinced that she had paid a debt due to Ann Blyth, or the tithe due for pasturing her horses. The £40 left to Thomas and Nathaniel were not in reality left to them. He made a strong objection to the payment of £40 to Nathaniel for the time he spent as a student at Cambridge University.

Bateman was an ambitious man who was determined to get his hands on every penny that his late wife should have had and was prepared to stir up trouble to get it. The court ignored all Bateman's allegations but made the executors increase their bond to £300 each and execute the terms of the will.[12]

Solicitors of the period could be as clever as any others in defrauding their clients to make provision for their own interests. Today a solicitor practising such deceit would be struck off the register. At this period, many solicitors were ill trained and were susceptible to temptation. Joseph and William Wood, father and son, were both involved in the will of Susan Crowther of Northowram in Halifax. William Appleyard, the heir to her estate, accused the Woods of tricking Susan Crowther into making her will in their favour and also appointing themselves as her executors. In fact, Joseph Wood was described as a solicitor who would 'frequently insinuate himself into the favour of Aged and infirm people under the pretence of drawing their securities and managing their affairs'. By using such means, Wood was able to obtain a distinct advantage for himself and his family.

After the death of her husband, Susan Crowther became 'a very aged woman and infirm, weak both in body and understanding, she being about eighty years of age'. Wood already knew that she possessed a fortune of some £3,000, so he resolved to employ every possible means he could to worm himself into her confidence.

Having succeeded, Wood began to put his plans into operation. First of all he motivated her against her relatives and especially Samuel Appleyard, her possible heir. Then he contacted all her closest relatives, telling them that he was really their friend and that he would attempt to advise her to make her will very much in their favour. He warned them that they must not approach her on the matter since she would become suspicious about their motives. Naturally, her relatives ceased to visit her as frequently as they had formerly done. The situation presented Joseph Wood with the opportunity to inform Susan that her relatives were neglectful.

His next step was to get Susan to entrust him with her will, and he warned her not to say anything to anyone except himself about how he intended to bequeath her estate, in case it should arouse arguments amongst her relatives. In due course the will was drawn up in accordance with Joseph Wood's plan. This was to ensure that by far the greater part of the £3,000 estate should be bequeathed to Joseph and his son William Wood, who were named as executors. The agreed witnesses were duly summoned: Jeremiah Swift, a whitesmith of Northowram, John Stocks, a mason of the same place, and Samuel Crowther, a shuttle bobbin maker from Sandshead in Northowram. They all agreed that they had seen the will and signed it as witnesses, but they had never heard it read over, although Swift believed that he was a legatee. In reality, the will was not that of Susan Crowther but of Joseph Wood, who had openly stated that he 'could make her will as he pleased and dispose of her estate as he wished'. This comment led Samuel Appleyard to remark that the will was obtained by 'fraud, false insinuations, indirect methods and practices'.

Some time afterwards, Susan Crowther fell ill and expressed a desire to set her affairs in order and divide her estate amongst her relatives. Accordingly she summoned Joseph Wood to attend her and set her affairs in order by preparing another will and having it legally executed. Although she sent for Wood several times, he prevaricated and made many excuses, until she became so ill that it was too late to do anything.

When she died, Wood began to make preparations for her funeral, but Nemesis struck and he too fell seriously ill and died; ironically Joseph Wood and Susan Crowther were both buried on the same day.

As death approached, Wood became haunted by the fear of Hell, so he repented and confessed that he had drawn the will contrary to the instructions of Susan Crowther, at the same time wronging Samuel Appleyard and his children as well as many others. Wood openly acknowledged that there were many other cases where he had drawn wills, writings and made bonds contrary to the instructions of the parties concerned. Although Martha Wood, Joseph's widow, and his son William were named as Susan Crowther's executors, the will was successfully challenged by Samuel Appleyard to the great satisfaction of Susan's relatives and friends.[13]

Another case where a shady solicitor attempted to obtain control of an estate, much as Wood had done in Halifax, comes from Silverdale in 1721. Richard Collinson challenged the claim by Richard and Maria Saul that Maria was the 'lawfull niece of Ellen Besbrown of Silverdale'. Collinson claimed that there were numerous relatives of the testatrix, 'all in nearer degree of kindred and who have a better title to administer the estate if the will can be rejected'.

Collinson's chief witness was one Thomas Evans from Clathropp near Burton in Kendal, who had been a boarder at Collinson's some five years previously. On one occasion, at Collinson's request, he accompanied him to visit Ellen Besbrown concerning her will, as he believed. While Collinson was engaged in his business, Evans went for a short walk. On his return he was summoned into the house where he witnessed, as he was requested to do, a paper in the presence of John Dale and Elizabeth Hutton, observing that Ellen Besbrown made her mark and did not sign the same. This being completed, Collinson took the document and they both left the house.

John Dale, speaking on behalf of Richard and Maria Saul, said he came to board with John Besbrown, where Ellen was also a boarder, and he had known them about eight years. On one occasion Collinson came to the house and produced a sheet of paper which he said was Ellen's last will, which he had witnessed with Thomas Evans and Elizabeth Hutton. Elizabeth expressed the opinion that she 'hoped it would do her no hurt'. Collinson replied, 'no hurt at all for it is only a writing betwixt aunt Ellen and myself'.

Dale was convinced that Ellen had no knowledge of the contents of the paper because, shortly after Collinson had left, Elizabeth Hutton enquired if Ellen had just signed her will. 'Was it your will?' she asked, to which Ellen gave a direct reply: 'God shil'd [forbid] it should be so for my will was made thirteen or fourteen years ago and I was then of perfect memory!' When Collinson had asked Ellen Besbrown to sign the document he called it a deed and said she must sign it, for it 'would do her no hurt', and then hand it back to him. Collinson's intention was, under the guise of a deed, to impose this document on her relatives by calling it her will. Ellen never assented to the writing or declared it as her will, for in reality she was afraid of Collinson who had all her effects in his custody.

Having signed the document, Ellen became dissatisfied and suspicious that she had signed the paper at Collinson's request without question. Confiding in Jennet Robinson what she thought she had signed, Jennet told her it could be her will. Ellen replied, 'God forbid, I made my will fourteen years ago', and added strong curses and imprecations to her remarks. Immediately, she sent for Collinson, who told her that her will was exactly as she ordered, but, in reality, he had drawn the will to suit his own interests. When Ellen died and the will came before the consistory court, the judge declared that Collinson was guilty for bringing 'an abominable and vexatious cause'. He was sentenced to pay full costs and was also excommunicated. The will was declared to be null and void.[14]

8

FALSE INVENTORIES

Dubious solicitors and executors were by no means the only persons who attempted to convert the assets of an estate to further their own interests and ignore those of the relatives. Executors were responsible for producing a true and reliable inventory of all the goods and chattels, movable and immovable, with each item valued as accurately as possible. Parties who opposed a will saw that the inventories could be used to claim that, in an attempt to defraud legatees of their rights, the various items were undervalued, so reducing the value of the expected legacy.

Richard Fish used this method to contest the inventory of John Rossall of Bispham produced by his son William. In the first place, Fish argued that the goods were falsely valued at £4.14s.4d., since he had bought the identical goods at the sale of John Rossall's goods. William Rossall confounded Fish's claim by confirming that the goods he bought were not £4.14s.0d. but only £1.4s.0d. Also, the goods mentioned by Fish as sold to Adam Stanhope were not delivered to him on the grounds that he was unable to pay for them. Therefore the goods were left in the house, but Fish removed them by breaking down a locked door.

Dorothy Fish, John Rossall's daughter, contested the claim made by William for expenses incurred in proving the will. She was quite convinced that 2s. per day was quite sufficient to cover the cost of William Rossall and his horse travelling to Pilling. Certainly no more than 8s. should be allowed for his journey to Lancaster.[1] The expenses were granted in accordance with William Rossall's claim and Fish was condemned in costs.

A case of disagreement between brother and sister occurred at

Fulwood in 1730, when Ellen Ryley, daughter of George Clayton, accused her brother William Clayton of presenting an incorrect inventory. Thomas Hodgson, a farmer of Ribbleton, stated that he had in his possession some cartwheels which belonged to George Clayton and must have cost at least £3. He offered to buy these from William Clayton for £2.8s.0d, but his offer was refused; William insisted on a price of £2.17s.0d., a sum Hodgson refused to pay.

Then there was the matter of Jane Clayton's annuity of 20s., payable twice a year. However, Jane had died in November 1728 and only one payment had been made.

Thomas Woodcock and William Oram of Walton had bought a black mare and a bay mare respectively from William Clayton for 45s. each, these having been George Clayton's horses. Oram also purchased twenty sheaves of oats and four sheaves of beans from William Clayton for 62s. in May 1728, which Clayton forgot to include in the inventory.

In addition, there was a matter of repairs to property. John Key, carpenter of Preston, was employed by William Clayton to repair a barn that was formerly George Clayton's at Fulwood. Under the terms of his father's will, William was also responsible for repairing a cottage. As matters turned out, someone else had repaired the barn, so when Key went to view the repairs, in company with three other carpenters to assess the cost, it appeared to them that the workmanship did not warrant more than 20s. to cover the cost. When Clayton was questioned about the cottage, he told the court that he had not undertaken any repairs, neither would he set a date for completion, on the grounds that the cottage 'was so precarious and the charges of reparation so great that he would obtain no benefit from undertaking the repairs'.

When it came to the matter of the sale of hay to William Craik, innkeeper of Preston, Craik said that he and a fellow innkeeper, Thomas Silcock, went to view the hay and made an offer of £7, but Clayton refused, saying he wanted a higher price. Silcock then offered to rent the Fulwood estate from Clayton for £6 per annum; the offer was rejected as being insufficient.

Thomas Shakeshaft, blacksmith from Preston, who had known the premises for many years, said that George Clayton died in 1727, when William Clayton took possession of the property. He owned the lands until he leased part of them for rent at £5 per annum; Clayton was to pay all taxes and see to repairs. He also referred to a debt of 14s. that Clayton owed him for work done. Neither had Ellen Ryley been paid her £10 for expenses incurred in connection with George Clayton's funeral. The court found William guilty of serious errors as an executor and sentenced him to pay the full costs of the dispute. In addition, Clayton was excommunicated for his negligence in not paying Ellen Ryley her lawful expenses.[2]

A creditor was often able to bring a successful action against an executor whom he suspected of illegality. Thomas Townson, who had kept an inn in Ulverston, made his wife Bridgett his sole executor. Giles Pepper, who was a substantial creditor, was suspicious that Bridgett was attempting to deceive the other creditors. He brought a suit into the consistory court on the grounds that she 'had produced a fictitious, fabricated, and imperfect inventory', for at the time of his death Thomas had a considerable estate in farm animals, corn, hay, silver, brass and pewter, which, with the rest of the household goods, was worth more than £3,000; the whole of this he bequeathed to his wife. In addition there was 'a fine and good Clock', together with a number of iron pots and pans, all of which were omitted from the inventory in order to defraud the creditors. Bridgett was compelled by the court to furnish a new inventory with each item recorded individually with its value, which, with the court fees, proved to be an expensive exercise.[3]

When George Walburne of Kirklington died in 1726, he left as his heir an infant daughter, who was placed in the care of George Barker, his executor, who had to act as guardian to the child. To his annoyance, Barker found himself being challenged by a creditor, George White, for his poor administration of the estate.

In his defence, George Barker said he did not believe that the items in the inventory were worth a great deal or that they could be sold for higher prices. The two cows were not worth more than £5. One had been sold, but the other had been in Barker's custody for three years and was not now worth £4, even if she had a calf with her. The calves mentioned in the inventory were worth no more than stated, which was about 20s. each. The value of the two draught mares was no more than £6, one having died within a short time of Walburne's death, being 'very old and scabbed', while the other was still with Barker. The best value that could be placed on the eighteen sheep was £6, for 'many were very mean and rotten, indeed most of them were now dead of rot'. The bed, bedstead, table and chairs were worth only 44s. and remained unsold.

George Barker denied that he had omitted any item concerning the personal estate of George Walburne from the inventory that came into his hands or indeed any other person's, intending to convert the same to his own use. He admitted that the clock was still in the possession of Mary Walburne, the widow, as was the pewter. The corn growing on the land and valued at £10 was harvested and stacked by Mary Walburne, who had also sold the unthreshed corn in the barn.

The deceased, according to Barker, left neither barley nor debts owing or due to him at the time of his death. The clock, the pewter and the crop of corn never came into his hands or those of any other person. He denied that he was responsible for these items and was certainly not compelled by law to sue for the same in court. He was quite satisfied that there was a debt of £20 due from Walburne to Richard Smith upon bond, which Barker had cleared by paying cash of £10 and giving his security for the balance. All the sums of money that he had paid out were *bona fide* payments.

George White took exception to the evidence and wanted each article itemized showing the value of each individual item. White was convinced that Barker had possessed himself of the goods and turned them to his own profit by selling them. White said that he stood in the 'circumstances of a creditor and was entitled to benefit from all Equity'. He found it impossible to convict Barker of perjury, although Barker had a 'loose, inefficient and evasive way of answering' questions. Though the individual items mentioned concerning horses, sheep and cattle might not be worth the sums stated, yet Barker should have recorded each individual item and its value, even if it was sold. White requested the court to order a proper assessment of the deceased's effects to be made so that he could recover his debt.[4]

An attempt to defraud Jane Armistead, a poor widow, of her rightful inheritance reveals the cupidity of some executors. In 1690, Jane Armistead brought a suit against Thomas Beckett, William Ellershaw and Christopher Ellershaw, executors of Thomas Proctor of Robert Hall in the parish of Tatham. Jane

Wildeman, a widow, said she had known Proctor for more than twenty years, for she had been a hired servant, and, further, 'that he was a very old man over eighty years of age, crazed in his memory and entirely unfit to make any will'. She also knew that the late Mrs Proctor had often expressed in public that 'she was unwilling to let him go abroad on any business by himself because he was easily imposed upon and to prevent this always sent Jane with him'.

After Mrs Proctor's death, Jane Wildeman married, becoming Mrs Beckett, and left Proctor's service. When he decided that he was unable to continue living on his own, Proctor came to live with Jane. About ten days before he died his mind failed; he recognized no one and no one came to visit him. On one occasion Thomas Beckett had visited Proctor at Robert Hall and discovered that he had not made a will. However, Jane remembered that one evening, as she was helping him into bed, he told her that he 'had not nor could not make any will'.

The day following Proctor's death, Christopher Ellershaw and Thomas Beckett, accompanied by Jane Talbot, a neighbour, came to see her for they were executors. Ellershaw produced a paper, which he handed to Jane Talbot, and asked her to read Proctor's will aloud, he having finally made one. The will was dated 1 January, which aroused Jane's suspicions because Proctor had not been out of the house on that day, neither did he make any will nor did any person call to see him that day. Indeed, Proctor regarded Ellershaw and Beckett as ordinary neighbours. His only living relative was Jane Armistead for whom he had great affection, saying that 'She should have whatever he left'.

One witness, Matthew Clapham, husbandman of Bentham, who was employed by the Revd Thomas Lupton, rector of Bentham, was drying oats at a kiln near Robert Hall when Proctor called in, saying 'he was cold', and sat by the fire to warm himself. During the conversation, Clapham asked what he intended to do with his money when he died, to which Proctor replied: 'I have a sister who is needful enough and she shall have a great share of what I have after I have served myself.' This was confirmed by Richard Colton, husbandman of Highgate, who had discussed the poor situation of Proctor's sister Jane with him. Proctor told him that 'he had a very great kindness and respect for her and she should have that sett her so she would not be beholden to anybody as long as she lived.'

Proctor's support for his sister was confirmed by Richard Iveson, linen weaver from Stainforth, who said that in the winter prior to his death Proctor came to see him at Ingleton when he asked him to take some money to his sister who was 'in some necessity'. When Iveson told him that he did well to consider his sister who was so poor, Proctor replied that 'she was his only living relative and he intended to do her good'.

Speaking on behalf of the executors, Richard Kendall, tailor of Low Bentham, said that he heard one James Bond, a relative of Robert Wildeman (Jane's brother) say that Wildeman had 'laid out five markes in money towards the management of this suit'. It appeared that Beckett was the prime mover in this cause. Robert Wildeman went to discuss with him Proctor's ability to make a will, for he was very old and deaf. Beckett went to visit Wildeman and, while walking together in a field behind the house, asked him to persuade Proctor to make a will. His reason was that Proctor would be prepared to give a goodly proportion of what he had to Beckett's wife Jane, who had been his servant, remarking 'I might as well have it if I can get it'.

Francis Beckett, yeoman of Tatham, said that in the previous September, while on his way to Hardicar, he met Jane Armistead who, during the course of conversation, told him she had been with the rector of Bentham consulting with him about a cause to be heard in the Richmond consistory. Moved by curiosity, he enquired as to the nature of the cause, whereupon she replied that she had a brother Thomas Proctor who 'had gott a Competent Estate by the Marriage of a widow that dyed before him and he was since dead'. She expressed the opinion that she considered Thomas Proctor had been unkind to her in leaving £80 in money and food but leaving her only 40s. a year if she should live so long. Jane was both grieved and disappointed, but she would not have taken the matter further because she could not afford the expense. It was Thomas Lupton, the rector, who persuaded her to proceed, following his consultation with Josias Lambert, a leading proctor in the Richmond court. Lambert advised her to go to Richmond and take out letters of administration. She promptly did as she was advised, and the rector paid the fees of 30s. in the presence of Robert Wildeman.

Wildeman told Jane that the bonds she required were in a chest at Robert Hall. All three went to Robert Hall and, acting on Wildeman's advice, she broke open the chest and removed the bonds in the presence of both men. They found two wills, one dated 1 January 1689 and the other the fifth of the same month in the same year. Lupton told her that 'he did not need to question but only twine the neck of the will about with such witnesses as he could produce', indicating that he was anxious to get the first will declared void.

Jane was to attend the court at Richmond, take her oath as a poor person (declaring that she 'was not worth five pounds') and leave the rest to Lambert and Lupton to manage. If the will was set on one side, Jane was to have only what they pleased and Wildeman was to have £8 for himself and his wife as witnesses' fees. The judge found that the second will was valid and the cause was settled in favour of Jane Armistead, while the executors had to pay costs.

When Michael Lanscale of Beethom died, his daughter, Margaret Couperthwaite, contested the will against the executor Thomas Hudson on the grounds that he had made an illegal distribution of the deceased's effects.

Thomas Johnson, speaking on behalf of Margaret Couperthwaite, said that Lanscale died owning:

1 black serge coat
2 doublets
1 cloth coat
2 pairs britches
3 pairs of stockings
1 pair of shoes
1 pair of boots and spurs
1 Rapier and Bolte
1 Fowling piece
1 chest

What the contents of the chest were he did not know, but several things were in the hands of Hudson. He knew these facts because he was a servant to Lanscale. He also believed that Margaret Couperthwaite had requested their return many times but Hudson had refused to return them.

A citation was served upon Johnson to get him to attend court. Upon his examination, he confirmed that there was 'great affection between Lanscale and Hudson'. Five days before he died, Lanscale asked for his cloak, and one day he reverted to the ancient medieval custom of giving seisin or possession of his goods by handing the cloak to Hudson, with the words: 'Here, Thomas, I give thee the cloak in lieu of all my goods.' By the simple action of handing over his cloak, Michael Lanscale meant that he had handed all his personal estate to Hudson, Johnson did not know if the deceased had a valid title to the goods. The judge declared the will valid by this action and Margaret Couperthwaite had costs to pay.[5]

Mary Lund and Elizabeth Boys were daughters of Robert Arkwright who accused his son John Arkwright, the executor, of producing a defective inventory in which the items were listed at 'far below current values' and 'divers goods and chattels wholly omitted'. The items in dispute were then listed:

> One black mare at forty five shillings, sold by the executor for six pounds.
> Corn in Turnhill and Meadow Hill, wheat, beans, oats I'th three Nook't Meadow valued at fifteen pounds is worth twenty.
> 5 loads of old Oats in the Garrett of the dwelling house sold for fifteen shillings and not accounted for.

It was also alleged that the deceased's clothing had been converted by the executor to his own use for £3. In addition he had taken turfs and canal coal worth 30s.

The funeral proved to be cheap, for the 'provision of the deceased and the presents of the neighbours' which were used meant that the cost was less than £4.

The charge brought was that the executor had made no attempt to include the debts owing. A proper inventory was ordered to be drawn up.[6]

Ann Topham, former wife of Godfrey Dawson of Coverham and executor of the will of Godfrey Dawson, brought a suit against her son Godfrey Dawson and his wife Maria concerning the inventory of her late husband's goods. Ann stated that the deceased's estate was worth between £10 and £300 at the time of his death on 30 January 1668.

The real problem was that the two Dawsons had seized all the deceased's goods and retained them. Ann Topham had demanded the return of all the goods removed, which were sheep, cattle, books, apparel and household goods of all kinds, as well as money due to the deceased, 'especially those mentioned in the schedule', to enable her to complete a correct inventory 'of the deceased's goods into the Registry to the end that she might pay the just debts and the funeral expenses of the deceased and such legacies as were given by the deceased according to her bond'.

The schedule that Ann complained about was as follows:

Deceased's purse and apparell   £6.13s.

1 Bible   10s.

1 Linen Tablecloth, 2 pairs of sheets, 3 coverlets, 6 table napkins, 3 towells   £3.12s.

2 planks, 11 boards, one table, one pann, 2 fanns, 3 chairs, 1 cheese press, 6 stools, 1 iron rake and other wooden vessels and huslement (junk and oddments)   13s.

1 paire of Gold weights   £6.0s.

In ready Coyne money, gold and silver   £50.0.0.

There was also one bond for the payment of £40 due to the deceased by John Dawson and unpaid when Godfrey Dawson died. Under a threat of greater excommunication, the Dawsons were ordered to surrender the goods and chattels to Ann Topham, the lawful executrix.[7]

The will of Thomas Greaves of Felkirk, husbandman, who died in 1717, was contested by his relatives Anthony and George Greaves against his widow Mary Greaves, alias Wood. The plaintiffs alleged that Mary Greaves had omitted several items from the inventory of her late husband's estate and that these were:

2 cows worth	£5
2 Heifers worth	£2
1 Hay Stack worth	£5.17s.
sheep worth	£4
a pan and brewing vessels worth	£1.10s.
Debt of Robert Hawley	£10

There were also many other items they considered to be much undervalued, such as his purse and apparel which were worth £3 and not £1. The prices should also be increased on pewter dishes, a cupboard, spoons, a brass pan, feather bed and bedding, and a chest.

There were several charges that should not be allowed, such as the funeral expenses of £4. The cost should only be £2 because what was provided was not worth £4, indicating a poor funeral feast. In addition, 12s. for a load of wheat and £1 for three strikes of malt, as well as a fee of £1 to Dr Drake, rural dean of Pontefract, for letters of administration should all be struck out. The deceased owed no debts, so all this shortfall should be charged to Mary Wood. The items of household stuff should also be charged to Mary Wood.

As so frequently happened, widows did not remain in that state for long, unless they were elderly or had little attraction, but remarried. Mary's first husband died on 2 November 1716, yet by the time the estate of her first husband was valued on 17 July 1717 she had married William Wood. In her reply, Mary Greaves alias Wood said that the haystack was worth only 50s. and that her cow, along with others lent by her father-in-law William Wood for the benefit of the milk, had eaten it. The heifers and sheep were also the goods of her father-in-law to William Wood. The brewing vessels and pan, so essential in a community where water was unsuitable for drinking, had been bought by her second husband Wood. The goods mentioned as being undervalued were offered to the plaintiffs at the prices mentioned but they had rejected the offer.

Mary Wood hoped that the court would allow the funeral charges, as well as the cost of the wheat and malt, which were debts owing by the deceased which she had paid, and also the fee to Dr Drake. The total value of her late husband's estate was £10.3s.2d., so Mary had effectively spent some £4.4s.10d. more than she received. The plaintiffs lost their cause and had to pay costs.[8]

The causes concerning mismanagement of an estate by executors often reveal the incompetence of these administrators in handling financial matters but also some psychological skill in handling difficult relatives.

9

DEBTS AND DEBTORS

Banking as we know it today and the financing of industry, agriculture and commerce did not exist in the seventeenth and early eighteenth century in the countryside. Country banks were beginning to appear, but the majority of people financed their operations through loans from friends and neighbours. West Riding clothiers in Marsden and Saddleworth, communities placed either side of the Pennines, financed their operations by borowing money on bond from each other. Often these sums were in the region of £200 or £300 but there is evidence in some inventories that amounts as large as £2,000 were involved. There was always the risk that by a sudden death or carelessness or some climatic seasonal cataclysm the debt could become impossible to recover, so bringing disaster both to the lender and to the borrower. Hence, debts and debt collection could be problems in many inventories, which were often challenged on the grounds that items of debt were omitted, either deliberately or in error.

An instance of this arose at Outrawcliffe in Garstang parish on the death of John Myerscough, a maltster of some standing. His widow, Marian Myerscough, and John Ashton, who was the executor, both claimed that the decreased was owed a considerable amount of money for malt sold to William Topping and his partner Roger Helme of Ingelwhite. Although Ashton admitted that he had received £9.10s.0d. from Topping for malt, Marian Myerscough insisted that the inventory was false because Ashton had omitted to include a debt owed by John Taylor of Garstang for six loads of malt, an additional two loads sold to Rosamund Butler totalling £4.8s.6d. and one load worth 15s. sold to 'one Caton a Romish priest'. (In this strongly

Catholic area the distinction between Protestant and Catholic counted for nothing where trading relations were concerned.)

Marian Myerscough did not believe that the debts incurred by William Pedder and Thomas Walmisley for malt were desperate, as Ashton claimed, but arose from wilful negligence in collecting the debts. Ashton also claimed that malt was sold by William Cornall, who had bargained with Rosamond Butler and John Taylor for the same, but they lived some 10 miles away and were not easy to contact.

Roger Helme of Garstang, speaking on behalf of William Cornall, said that Myerscough was a joint partner with him in the lease of a malt-drying kiln and he had agreed with Myerscough to pay him his proportion of the lease when it was due. Ashton appears to have been reluctant to collect the debts in person, and desired to be rid of the whole business. Indeed, he made an offer to sign over his interest in the estate to Marian Myerscough, who, being a very determined woman, was prepared to go to any lengths to recover the debts in full.[1]

Another who found difficulty in balancing the accounts of her deceased husband was Margaret Winter of Cockerham, widow of the vicar who had died in 1772. She admitted that she had managed to pay his debts, which amounted to £25.11s.9d. for malt. The wages of John Bryning, his servant amounting to £4.2s.0d. were paid at Candlemas, a northern quarter day, and John Walker was paid £1.6s.0d. for work done during the vicar's lifetime, in the meantime, she had sold a cow to Edward Gardener for £4.3s.4d. and paid 2s. for cloth to James Beaumont, to make herself a pair of stockings. Knitted woollen ones had not yet replaced the older peasant style of using cloth for this purpose. She had also paid Peter Cook £16s. for beef 'had and used in the vicar's lifetime'. In addition there were payments to Joshua Hodgson for wheat and the grazing of a cow, to which was added the cost of the funeral at £5 – a charge that she considered somewhat heavy. Overall, Margaret Winter claimed to have paid out £3.8s.0d. more than she had received and was anxious to recover the balance by means of a court order.[2]

Accidental death and the deceased leaving no will could and did create problems, as in the case of John Baguley of Oldham who died in 1662. According to the evidence of Robert Lees of Chorlton, a Linen weaver, John Baguley died 'suddenly by a fall into a cole pitt one might without any will made'. Lees was present when the rural dean of Manchester granted letters of administration to his widow, Margaret, and also when the goods of the deceased were valued; William Hunter of Manchester was present at the same time.

It soon became clear that Baguley was indebted to a number of creditors, the principal one being Hunter. He said that 'the Bellman of Manchester was paid one shilling to announce in public that there would be a meeting of the creditors'. At the same time a certificate was 'put out of the parish church to satisfy the creditors in Yorkshyre'. At their meeting the creditors agreed that Hunter, as the principal creditor, should be responsible for the collection of all the debts owing and divide the proceeds, including the money raised by the sale of Baguley's effects, to the satisfaction of the creditors.

Lees stated that some £24 was owing to the deceased, but he had no idea of the value of the small items, except the deceased's clothes, which were valued at 17s. The day following the valuation and before letters of administration were taken out, Hunter had removed everything from the house, except one bed which he left for Margaret Baguley. He then proceeded to dispose of the remainder at his leisure.

Once she had been appointed as the official administrator, Margaret went to see Hunter and demanded the return of all the deceased's goods so that she could sell them and pay out the creditors. Hunter refused point blank to do so. The valuation of the goods (two horses, some hay, two flagons and a pair of looms) was only £12; all were sold by auction, including the household stuff. Edmund Mellor, a weaver from Oldham, confirmed the valuation and said that he had bought the deceased's clothes for 17s.

Further evidence was provided by William Hamson, whitster, of Pendleton, who confirmed that he had bought a great pan from Hunter for 25s. He had also received, when on business in York, £3 'of some persons who were indebted to the deceased'. He knew what Hunter had done in the matter of the estate.

In her accounts Margaret showed that she had received £4.18s.2d., out of which she had paid 6s.8d. for the letters of administration and £1 for the funeral, which, at that price, would not justify a feast. She then added on the cost of the cause pending in the consistory court, but realized that the legal dues of £5.18s.4d. would fall far short of what would be required. Margaret requested that Hunter should be 'publicly denounced and declared excommunicate' for his actions and refusal to recognize her rights. Hunter was ordered to make some restitution to Margaret Baguley.[3]

In 1717, Mary Cooke of Gloucester challenged James Robbins about the will of James Robbins deceased. She was concerned about the many goods and chattels that were omitted from the inventory. She was also concerned that no more money was due from James Robbins than the £106 which he had discharged in the inventory. She considered that bad debts and desperate debts ought to be included, especially a debt of £8 due from Alderman Niccols, although he was in circumstances which made him unable to pay it. Further, Niccols was indebted to the deceased under a bond of £30 plus interest. All she could recover of the bond was £20 plus interest.

There was also a debt of £11 due from Dorcas Matthews who 'was so poor and necessitous during the lifetime of the deceased and he advanced from time to time so much money for her support and at the time of his father's death Dorcas was indebted more than double her share of the said estate'. James Robbins hoped that the items for wine and cake for the funeral would be allowed. He did not order more than the estate would bear, so he invited very few of his father's friends to the funeral.[4] The recovery of money out on loan or bond could be difficult at times. Many city aldermen were both borrowers and lenders, taking a great deal of financial risk which sometimes ended in financial disaster.[5]

10

LEGACIES AND BEQUESTS

The sections in any will that are likely to provide revenue for the legal profession are those which deal with legacies and bequests, for families could, and still do, make these contentious. Since these legacies and bequests name the legatees concerned, it becomes possible to reconstruct a record of family relationships, which can assist in compiling a family tree.

In July 1709, Anna Sober, widow of Richmond and executor of the will of Grace Hutchinson, brought a cause against John Smith concerning a legacy purported to have been left to her by Grace, and whether the original will had been lost or deliberately destroyed. Edward Smithson, gentleman of Richmond and executor of the will of Grace Hutchinson, stated that on 22 November 1708/9 Thomas Dickenson, an attorney at law who was Smithson's employer, handed him a paper which purported to be the last will and testament of Grace Hutchinson. He ordered Smithson to make a correct copy and deliver the same to the house of Samuel Fisher in Richmond. When he arrived at the house, he found not only Grace but also Mrs Sober. He took both women into a room in Fisher's house where he read the will to them and enquired if it was drawn 'according to her mind'. Grace agreed and he went on to state that he had found her in good health and of a 'sound mind and disposing memory'. Also present on that occasion were Samuel Fisher and Anna Jackson, who both heard the will read over and then witnessed it.

Samuel Fisher, mercer of Richmond, said that when he saw Grace on 22 November last she was of sound memory and approved the will when it was read over to her. Samuel said he had known Grace for many years before her death. He also knew that Mr Smith and Mrs Sober were relatives of Grace Hutchinson and he had been informed that they paid Grace an annual sum of money for her maintenance during her lifetime.

Fisher also recalled that when Nicholas Markendale was on his deathbed he requested Fisher to take care of his effects until his brother arrived. Fisher kept his promise and, when going through Markendale's papers with his brother, they found the sealed will of Grace Hutchinson. Immediately, he took it to her, read it over with her and confirmed that this was really her will. She requested Fisher to take care of it, but what happened to it between that time and Grace's death he 'knew not except that Mr Smith and Mrs Sober were named as executors', 'neither did he know what legacies had been left to them'!

Ten days before the date on the will, Grace came in the company of Mrs Sober to Samuel Fisher's shop and requested him to draw up her will. He took down what she dictated and sent it to Mr Dickenson to be drawn in proper form. It seemed clear to him that Grace was not under any influence, as John Smith alleged, to make her will in the manner she did. Dickenson drew up the will, which contained no more than Grace had dictated to Fisher. The final version was read over to her in her own dwelling house where she was sitting. John Smith's allegations were disproved and the will was declared valid by the judge.[1]

In 1723, Robert Butterworth, curate of Woodplumpton, was cited into court to prove the will of William Salisbury deceased at the request of Sarah Hornby of Roseacre, Salisbury's sister. Butterworth, who had drawn up the will, claimed that Salisbury was in a sensible frame of mind in his last illness when he, in the presence of Robert Moon and others, read over the will to him, which was then approved and sealed by Salisbury. That being concluded, Butterworth then handed over the will to Sarah Hornby for safe keeping. Whether or not she had destroyed it or lost it he did not know, but he could not produce it. In any case, the estate was inconsiderable, for Salisbury was only a weaver and so his goods were never valued.

Butterworth sold the looms to John Brown for £35 and he handed the money over to Sarah Hornby. Robert Moon, also a weaver, saw Salisbury sign the will in the presence of Joseph Fidler and both believed that the estate of William Salisbury was worth no more than £10. It was clear that Sarah had converted many of Salisbury's goods to her own use. She believed that Salisbury had left more than there really was. Poor Butterworth got his knuckles well and truly rapped by the judge for not having produced a correct inventory of Salisbury's goods with a true valuation of each item, and for not taking out letters of administration. The poor curate had, for his negligence, to pay the full costs of the cause.[2]

John Muchett of Lindale in Cartmel challenged the will of his father John, who was a prosperous yeoman, on the grounds that it was a fictitious one because the deceased had appointed his widow Mary as his sole executor and nothing had been left to his son. Naturally John Muchett was annoyed that he was left out of the will, but Mary Muchett said the will was signed in the presence of William Kellet, George Preston and Miles Croft, who witnessed the will. George Preston confirmed that the deceased was, at the time he made his will, of a perfect and disposing mind and memory, but, alas, he lived only four days after the will was signed.

William Kellet, yeoman of Lindale, was also present when the will was signed but, speaking on the side of John Muchett the son, declared that it was not read over to the deceased in the presence of the witnesses. The weight of evidence was on the side of Mary, for had not the deceased 'bequeathed all his real and personal Estate' to his wife. The judge declared that the will and testament was a valid one.[3]

Isabella Moore was a determined spinster who was convinced that she had been defrauded of her expectations under the will of John Johnson of Kirby Lonsdale who died in 1710. When questioned about his signature to the will, James Bordrigge of Whittington, yeoman, confirmed that the signature was his own but 'at what time, date or place or for what reasons he subscribed as a witness he cannot now recall'. Nevertheless, some three years previously John Johnson was 'seized with some sudden fitte by which he became lame and speechless'. Receiving a summons to attend Johnson he went and found that he, together with Richard Cort and Christopher Ellershaw, were to be witnesses. He was surprised to discover that Johnson, although speechless, was able to hear and understand what was said to him. Asking if Cort and Ellershaw were to be witnesses, Johnson indicated that 'he had made such his will and they were witnesses thereto', at which Johnson seemed very well pleased.

William Bordrigge of Kirby Lonsdale, mercer, affirmed that he and Johnson had been very close friends for over twenty years and he had frequently been present when Johnson was writing letters. Asked to inspect the will dated 14 November 1706 he confirmed that the handwriting and signature were both those of Johnson. He was quite convinced that Johnson had written the will because he had several documents in his possession which he truly believed that Johnson wrote. He had been comparing the writing on the documents with that of the will 'by observing the Characters, the Breakes, strokes & Cutts of the Letters therein, the handwriting is that of John Johnson'. He continued his evidence by pointing to the existence of a common fame and report in Kirby Lonsdale that Johnson 'before he became speechless and disordered by a fitt of the palsy had fully intended to marry Isabella Moore, the party promoting the cause'.

Simon Battersby of Biggins, a yeoman, was often present in the room where Johnson lay after 'his distemper of Lameness & being so speechless', and confirmed that, despite his affliction, Johnson could understand what was spoken to him. Whenever the will was discussed, he was always pleased when the names of Cort, or Ellershaw or Bordrigge were named as witnesses.

Some six months before Johnson died, Richard Cort, who was a friend of long standing, went to visit him. His purpose was to find out if Johnson had named him as a witness. Cort asked Johnson that, if the intention that he should act as a witness was correct, 'then he hoped Johnson would give him his hand as a sign or token of it'. In response, Johnson 'took him by the hand and shaked his hand and Clapped him upon his Shoulders and smiled'. By this action Cort understood that Johnson had made his will and that he was to be a witness.

Christopher Ellershaw of Tatham Fell, also a yeoman, believed that 'he was a fit and proper person to attest his will', by reason of the good friendship and intimacy that had always existed between them. Indeed, he would not have subscribed as a witness had he not been satisfied that the will was signed and sealed by Johnson as his own action.

Another friend of long standing was Thomas Harling of Kirby Lonsdale, who had receipts from Johnson in his own handwriting. He compared the handwriting of the receipts with that of the will and both were identical. Incidentally, none of the three witnesses had anything to say about Johnson's nephew, John Winder, who seems to have been regarded as Johnson's heir but was an extremely unpleasant young man, as will be noted.

Jane, the wife of Rowland Wallas of Kirby Lonsdale, said that the previous Christmas, Isabella Moore, the executrix, came to their house where Johnson was a lodger. Cort came on a visit and Isabella asked him into the room where Johnson lay, 'speechless and lame'. Isabella then handed the will to Johnson, who opened it with his left hand and handed it to Cort, who signed as a witness. When he had done this, Johnson took him 'by the hand and smiled' being pleased that he had 'owned his handwriting'.

Jane believed that if Johnson had not been seized 'with such a Distemper which made him incapable of Matrimony, he would have married Isabella'. For some time it appeared that Johnson had been courting her with a view to marriage and there was every indication that he would have done so if he had not been struck down with the palsy. Jane Wallas went on to say that she had seen Johnson very angry with John Winder, his nephew. She had observed that Johnson showed that he was both displeased and uneasy when he was in his nephew's company, both before and after he was afflicted with the palsy. The reason for his attitude was Winder's extravagance and bad management of his uncle's affairs. The judge gave his verdict in favour of Isabella Moore.[4]

Some persons appear to have been most reluctant to make a will, doubtless maintaining the belief that when a will has been made it has the same effect as signing a death warrant. Hence the drawing of a will is delayed as long as possible, often to a time when it is almost too late, for death is imminent.

A good illustration of this comes from Melsonby in 1698, concerning the will of Cuthbert Burrell. John Burrell, his son, stated that he had frequently urged his father during his illness to make a will, but he always received the same reply, 'next week or the week following' would do. A few hours before his father died John went to Barton Cuthberts to ask Thomas Gyll to come and draw his father's will. However, when they returned to the house they found Cuthbert so very weak and 'his capacity and understanding much impaired by reason of his long indisposition and great sickness' that there was little that could be done. During the time that Thomas Gyll was present Cuthbert said nothing, neither did he take any notice of what was going on around him. John Burrell had no alternative but to dictate to Thomas Gyll what he should write as minute for the will.

After both men had departed, Cuthbert began to reflect upon what he had said to John in answer to his questions and he decided, in the presence of several witnesses, that what had been put into writing should not be his will. If that happened, both his wife and children would become beggars, having a house to build upon the premises for themselves because the present house went to John as his heir.

Elizabeth Burrell, his widow, decided to contest the will on the grounds that it did not express the mind of her late husband. In his father's defence, John Burrell said that, when he went for Thomas Gyll, his father was of sufficient understanding and quite capable of making a will to dispose of his effects. His father gave no orders beyond bequeathing £20 to his sister White. Thomas Gyll went away to draw the will but when he returned three hours later the deceased was in no condition to execute it. Cuthert Burrell made no comment during the drawing of the will and John certainly never dictated anything to his father. The judge declared in favour of the widow since her situation was unjust as it stood, so Elizabeth was given a share of the estate.[5]

Those left without a legacy, especially if they were close relatives, usually did their best to get the situation changed. James Burley of Neenham, Gloucester, who died in 1717 made the fatal mistake of omitting his sister Anne Lovell from his will. Thomas Hyett of Newnham, gentleman, said that James Burley sent for him on the previous 13 June to make his will. In the evening of that day, he went to see Burley who gave him instructions and directions how to draw his will, which he did in the will now exhibited in court. When the will was read over to the testator, he declared himself satisfied and proceeded to set his seal and his mark to the same, while John White attested it by signing his name.

Hyett stated that he had known Burley for seven years and above, since he lived only 3 miles away. When Burley sent for him to make his will, he was visiting his father who lived 'a mile and a half' away from Burley. Although he conversed with the deceased he had no idea of his age. He died within a week of making his will. Hyett believed that Burley acted freely in the affair, since he expressed satisfaction with it and, when he asked him who should have custody of it, he replied that Tom Ambrose, his executor, should have it and not his sister. He knew that Burley had not left anything to his sister in his will.

John White of Blakeney, wool merchant, said that on the 'Thursday before Whitsunday last' he saw James Burley sign his will 'by writing his Name before the Seale' and heard Hyett ask him if he was satisfied with it. He with Anne Meare and Thomas Hyett witnessed the will. He confirmed that he had known the testator 'from his Youth and lived in the neighbourhood' where the testator lived. He had not had much conversation with him over the years except when they were either coming or going to the market.

Anne Meare of Blakeney said that the previous Whitsuntide she saw Hyett come into the room where James Burley lay sick. She left the room while the will was drawn, but Burley saw her witness it. She had lived with Burley for three years acting as his servant, but had no idea as to his age. Burley refused to have the will read over to him or to the witnesses. She thought that Anne Lovell as his only sister should have had a legacy. The judge decreed that, as his only close relative, she should have a share of the estate.[6]

An excellent illustration of the tensions that could exist within a family is to be found in the will of William Baskerville of Sound in the parish of Acton, which was contested by Elizabeth Baskerville, his widow, and Margaret Ely, formerly Baskerville his daughter, against Thomas Baskerville and Ralph Cheyney the executors. It appears that the deceased had granted and bequeathed to Elizabeth, his wife, one-third of all the household stuff, goods, cattle, implements, corn and debts owing to him to the value of £20 per annum during her widowhood.

The deceased had only one child, a daughter Margaret, 'whom he did dearly love and respect . . . declaring that his Estate was all too little for her if he were worth a thousand pounds'. When Margaret married John Ely her father had given her no marriage portion, although her husband 'was of good reputation and of a clear and considerable Estate and doth maintain a good rank and quality'. This was clearly the sort of marriage any father of the period would have welcomed. It is evident that tensions already existed between father and daughter when he openly refused to increase the legacy he had bequeathed to Margaret and would make no other will, for he had 'no good liking or favour to the said Margaret Ely who was his daughter'.

Ann Jenwall, widow and sister of William Baskerville, said that 'for eight or nine weeks before his death she was constantly at his house with him in his sickness. If any came to see him, he insisted that she or her daughter should be with him'.

No doubt this was a precaution against pressure from any interested parties being put upon him to change his will.

The morning preceding his death, Thomas Powell came to see him and naturally enquired if he had settled his estate. Baskerville replied 'Yes', adding that he had left some legacies to poor friends. However, when Powell asked if he had left or made any provision for his wife and daughter, Baskerville replied 'No', but he had settled it upon his wife. No other parties were present on this occasion except Jane Blagg, who left and refused later to confirm that the deceased had changed his mind.

Although Powell had urged him to change his mind, Baskerville refused. There was gossip in the locality that Margaret was not the lawful daughter of Baskerville or taxable for half the deceased's estate, but Powell did not intend that such words should warrant the will being revoked. Clearly at some earlier date there had been a serious quarrel between Baskerville and his wife as well as his daughter. His wife had left him and Margaret left to be married. However, during his last illness his wife had returned and they did 'live lovingly together'.

Robert Wright, gentleman of Nantwich, came to see Baskerville on 7 February, but found him weak and sick. After some very earnest conversation, he prevailed with the deceased to do 'something more for his daughter,' which he did by adding a codicil to the will. This was added to the foot of the will by William Meakin, who then read it out to the deceased, who signed it in the presence of Meakin and his servant Michael Tilly.

John Moore, husbandman, who had been thatching a roof at Broomhall Green, came on 14 March, the day that Baskerville died. Baskerville declared to him that the 'estate should go to Elizabeth Baskerville and his daughter Margaret Ely'.

Michael Tilly, Baskerville's servant, provided an important

clue when he revealed that Baskerville had had a serious quarrel with his daughter but that they were reconciled shortly before he died. Indeed he was with the deceased when Margaret came to see her father, who told her that she 'could have everything except a mare which he wished Mr Wilbraham to have' and hoped that his wife and daughter would agree; this they did and the will was authenticated and proved.[7]

The dispute between Anthony Moore and Thomas Patrickson of Foulyate, who was the sole executor of Henry Moore, reveals a complete lack of Christian love and charity, but at the same time provides a reference to education in the locality. Henry Moore lived at Starmine in St Bees parish and he had become a close friend of Thomas Warrall, a yeoman of High Walton. The two had first met when both were pupils at Goosebutts school in St Bees. Pupils had to take their midday lunch with them to school and Worrall used to leave his lunch at Henry Moore's house. As he had occasion to go into the house quite frequently, he became closely acquainted with him.

A few days before the will was drawn up, Worrall was suddenly summoned by Ann Cook of High Walton to go to Moore's house. He went and found him in bed. Henry Moore told him that 'he little thought that he would have been in that condition since he last saw him in May [1749]', saying that he wished to change his will. Enquiring what changes Henry wanted to make, Henry replied that the legacy of 20s. which 'he had left to his landlord Lancelot Bouch sho'd be quite left out and that the legacies he had left to the Children of his half brother Anthony Moore should be paid to the Children only and not their father'. The amended will was executed in the room where the deceased lay in bed and John Hutchinson and himself subscribed their names in the presence of Thomas Patrickson.

Worrall also confirmed that, in his opinion and that of many others, Henry Moore's stepbrother Anthony Patrickson was a poor man whose character was somewhat pathetic. Indeed there was very little sign of any intimacy and friendship between Moore and his stepbrother. He had heard Moore say that Anthony should have nothing of any value that belonged to the deceased. In any case, Patrickson was in no way a direct relation to Moore. The amended will was accepted and proved.[8]

Family relationships often lay at the root of a desire for a testator to change his will. John Hodgson of Little Layton decided in 1730, while on his death bed, to amend the legacies he had bequeathed. At his death, John Hodgson left a widow, Elizabeth, three daughters and five sons. Richard Tennant of Poulton, gentleman, said that on 10 May last, James Hodgson came to ask him to come and amend his father's will. When he arrived he found John Hodgson sitting in the bodystead or living room of his house and both then went into the parlour. It appeared that Hodgson wished to reduce the legacies he had bequeathed to his daughters from £40 each to £30, and at the same time to advance the legacies to his sons, Joseph, Thomas, Benjamin, Ralph and Jonathon from £5 to £10 each. The amended will was read over to the testator and duly executed, with James and Joseph appointed as executors.

In the course of his evidence concerning this amended will, George Hodgson stated that Ralph Hodgson was a minor about 16 years of age. He continued his evidence by stating that, while he was on his way to church on Sunday 10 May last, he was met by Jane Hodgson, who asked him to 'come and change her father's will'. Since a second witness was required to sign the amended will, Henry Archer, a neighbour of Little Layton, was called in to act. Meanwhile, George Hodgson and Thomas Sanderson waited in the living room or bodystead of the house until they were summoned by the testator's wife. Archer said that he saw the testator sitting upon his bed and observed Tennant hand him the amended will to sign, which he did with extreme difficulty. Having done this, the testator made his affirmation in public. George Hodgson maintained that his father was of perfect mind and sensible when he 'came out of the Chamber into the Bodystead of the House . . . and the deceased's wife taking hold of his arm, sat him down in the great Chair by the fireside'. On the last night of John Hodgson's life, George sat with his father, who was sensible and 'smoked his pipe very cheerfully'. During the conversation, the testator handed his pipe to George that he might share it, a custom that was usual in some rural areas. It is clear that the relationships between the deceased and his daughters were very strained.[9]

11

THE CHILD'S PORTION

One source of trouble that could be aroused by any will was that relating to the child's portion. In 1712, when William Gregg of Hawkshead died, his will gave rise to a dispute of this nature. In the first place, Reginald Gregg denied that he was the executor for his father's will; he had therefore refused to interfere with either the goods or the personal estate left by his father. In reality, it was Agnes Gregg, his mother, who was the true executrix.

The root cause of this dispute concerned the lands left to Jane Gregg, a daughter of the deceased, who was now the wife of Peter Lickbarrow. In June 1712 the matter was referred to Mr Wren of Castlerigg and William Atkinson of Cartmel, for it was Peter Lickbarrow who opposed the will of his father-in-law. He made reference to a letter which purported to have come from Ireland giving proof that his wife Jane, one of the heiresses of William Gregg, was not dead but still alive. Naturally, he never took out any letters of administration for her goods because he knew that she was alive.

The legacy bequeathed in lands to Jane was intended for the male heirs of the testator, which in default of a male heir was to go to his daughters, reserving Jane's share 'if she is dead to her heirs and not the administrators'. A letter from Robert Satterthwaite to Peter Lickbarrow insisted that Reginald Gregg should show just cause 'why he could not have his wife's portion which was one of seventeen pounds out of the land which her other sister had retained'. Satterthwaite also warned Lickbarrow not to let his ambition become master, for 'he should not make himself so large and benefit by selling the lands'. Since Lickbarrow had married the elder sister, then she should have a full and the best share of the estate. The advice given was to pursue a cause in the consistory court and have the estate valued without delay. Unfortunately the full cause file is lost and only the final decree survives that Jane Lickbarrow received her full share of the estate.[1]

In 1690, Alice Sharp was appointed administrator of the estate of John Crawford of Wrayton in Melling parish. Alice was the sister of John Crawford and his only close relative apart from his mother Ann Crawford, who was still alive. Ann Crawford made up her mind to see that, whatever happened, she would ensure that the child of her daughter Alice Sharp would receive its child's portion.

Accordingly Ann summoned Henry Battye, the schoolmaster of Warton Grammar School, to draw up the requisite legal documents to ensure the child received the portion due to it. At this period, schoolmasters had many sidelines and one of them was the ability to draw deeds of conveyance of property. This kind of legal business enabled schoolmasters to augment their stipends, which were by no means generous.

In response to her request, Battye drew up a deed of bargain and sale to John Crawford 'of all her goods, chattels, household stuff and implements and the money in her possession'. Ann Crawford knew that her son John was heavily in debt and his debts could not be cleared before he died. Under the terms of the deed it was agreed that John Crawford should pay the child of Alice Sharp £30; the deed was duly signed and sealed.

To ensure that the money should be available, various sums were collected for this purpose. William Stackhouse of Burton in Kendal obtained a receipt from William Redmayne for 5 guineas. Francis Sharp gave a receipt for 30s. and Margaret Sharp another one for a similar amount, while Thomas Wildman gave security for 10 guineas in order to raise the £30 required for the child of Alice Sharp, since John Crawford did predecease his mother.[2]

It was by no means uncommon for money set aside to pay a child's portion to be borrowed and used for the purposes of a loan to a second party. The cause of Fletcher Crosby is a good illustration of this practice. It appears that Anne Crosby had lent the money set aside for her child's portion and now required the loan to be repaid. In her petition, Jane

Crosby stated that Anne Crosby was her mother and she was the daughter of Anthony Crosby and the same person to whom a legacy of £20 had been bequeathed. Details of family relationships were provided by Richard Jackson, vicar of St Bees:

Anne, daughter of Anthony Crosby of Sandwith baptised
  28 September 1690
Jane Crosby (sister) buried 12 November 1708
Anthony Crosby (father) buried 27 April 1712
Anne Fletcher formerly Crosby buried 27 August 1721.

Elizabeth Cook of St Bees, aged 70, said that she called at Joseph Walker's house in Sandwith some two years before the previous Martinmas on her way to Whitehaven, when John Fletcher, his wife, Anne, and Jane Crosby, the defendant, were all present in the house. It was revealed during the course of conversation that Jane Crosby had lent to Mary Bolton, widow, £20 and she was now asking for the return of this money since it was really the property of her daughter Anne, being her child's portion, and naturally she preferred cash to a bond.

Joseph Walker of Sandwith, while walking home from his work some eighteen months ago, met Jane Crosby at Sidelands. During the conversation he had with her it was revealed that she now needed the £20 which she had lent to his mother-in-law Mary Bolton, a sum which she was now liable to pay since John Fletcher and her daughter Anne were 'buying a house in Whitehaven'.

James Dawson, stonemason of Sandwith, declared that early in the previous October, at the request of John Fletcher, he accompanied James Wycliffe to demand from Jane Crosby his wife Anne's child's portion, which he had never received but he expected that Jane Crosby would pay the sum due.

In response to their request, Jane Crosby replied in a loud voice, 'I shall never pay any more than I have already paid'. During the conversation Jane was adding up a number of small sums of money that her daughter Anne had lent to others after her marriage to John Fletcher. She claimed that the £10 that was said to be in the house when Anne Fletcher died was part of her child's portion. James Dawson replied by stating that the 'ten pounds might be her Husband's', since he was a mariner who was engaged in trade with Virginia. In fact, Dawson believe that:

> the money she lent out since her marriage was no part of her portion nor the money in the house at the time of her death (if any) but money which her husband left with her for he never took any money with him to Virginia.

John Fletcher indeed had money of his own, and both he and Anne were a very loving couple who kept nothing from each other.

James Wycliffe confirmed that he accompanied Dawson to interview Jane Crosby on the matter. When she refused Dawson's request, Wycliffe asked her if she had any discharge for the money from her daughter, to which Jane replied sharply 'No'. He then advised her to meet John Fletcher, her son-in-law, and try to arrive at a settlement. Clearly relationships between Jane Crosby and John Fletcher were not harmonious, for she replied with some acrimony 'I have no business to meet him'. Wycliffe then informed Jane Crosby that the sum of £5 was due to John Fletcher, her son-in-law, on the death of his wife's sister Jane. Jane Crosby, the mother, sharply denied that this money was due and they parted acrimoniously.

The last witness was Mary Crosby, spinster of Sandwith, who admitted that she was present when a legacy of £21 was paid to Anne Crosby, her sister, before her marriage to John Fletcher, by Dacre Pow who was Mary's uncle. This payment was intended to be in full discharge of her child's portion under the will of Anthony Crosby, but she gave no receipt, neither was one requested. Also present when the legacy was paid were Robert Crosby, mariner, Stephen and Henry Crosby. Jane gave Dacre Pow a bond for £21 stating that he owed this sum to Jane Crosby.

Mary also said that several times, both before and after her sister's marriage to John Fletcher, she had heard Anne say that she had received the legacy now sued for and as a result was able to lend money to her neighbours. A sum of £15 was lent to Robert Crosby and a further £4 to Mary Atkinson, now the wife of Joseph Rudge, for which she accepted a trunk and a piece of cloth as security.

For most of the time before her marriage, and indeed for one year afterwards, Anne lived with her mother and was never in domestic service, neither had she any visible means of support, so she was maintained by her mother, as all the neighbourhood well knew. Mary was unable to name the month and year of her father's death, but remembered that Jane died one year before her father.

Robert Crosby remembered Dacre Pow, his father-in-law, paying Anne Crosby the legacy some three years prior to her marriage, a payment which she accepted but gave no receipt for. Mary, Stephen and Henry were all present at the time. He said that Anne had lent him £15 from her legacy, which he had since repaid.

Jane Crosby died before she attained her majority, so the £20 she was due to receive was divided between the survivors in the sum of £5 each. The promotor of the cause, John Fletcher, requested that the court would sentence Jane Crosby, the executrix of Anthony Crosby, to pay the £20 left to Anne as her portion, with interest added from the time the money became due. This was not awarded by the court, which sentenced Jane Crosby to pay the money due and costs.[3] Relatives by marriage have changed but little in their attitudes, for many are no more co-operative in the twentieth century than their ancestors were in the eighteenth.

From time to time attempts were made to influence executors, as occurred in the case of Alexander Parker of Lickhurst in Bowland. Parker made his will on 4 November 1725, when he appointed John Parkinson of Chipping and John Parker of Bowland as his executors.

Thomas Dilworth, father and guardian of Ellis Dilworth, a minor, contested the will on the grounds that Ellis Dilworth ought to have inherited a large part of the estate of the deceased since he was closer in relationship to the deceased than any other. However, he said that the deceased was incapable of making a will, on the grounds that 'he had become afflicted with a dumb palsy' before he could give directions about his will. The judge told Parker that he had been 'inadvertently advised' when asked to become an executor of the will of Alexander Parker. The validity of the will was upheld and Dilworth sentenced to pay full costs for his attempt to influence the executors.[4]

Problems could arise from time to time in the administration of an estate, especially where renunciation was involved. One such case began in 1677 when Joseph Fourness died and left the administration of his estate in the hands of Abraham Brigg and Abraham Hall. However, the personal estate of Joseph proved to be insufficient to meet his debts and legacies, so these had to be met from his real estate.

By 1710 the estate, which was valued at £570, came into the hands of John Fourness, both the original administrators being dead. John Fourness entered into possession of an estate and farm called Brackenbed Grange in Ovenden in which Joseph Fourness had originally had an interest. When John died he bequeathed Brackenbed Grange and his personal estate to his widow, Frances Fourness, formerly Oats, and made her his sole executrix.

Shortly after her husband's death, Frances Fourness married Gabetis Norton, who promptly settled lands on her as a marriage portion in order to provide her with an income should he die before she did. By this act Gabetis Norton obtained an interest in Brackenbed Grange. Then Gabetis appointed three of his nephews, Philip Lander, William Kay and the Revd Thomas Kay, together with Edward Norton as his executors. When this case commenced in 1765, only two executors survived – Thomas Kay and Philip Lander. They were still acting as administrators. The estate had come into the control of John Fourness, grandson of Joseph. From the evidence given, it appeared there were other descendants alive who also had a claim to the estate.

Joseph's daughter, Martha, had married Samuel Livesy, who gave evidence on behalf of Jonathon Martin, a merchant who was a creditor, who maintained that his title to Brackenbed Grange was never released to anyone or mentioned in any renunciation. Livesy said he was 65 years old and that the 'winding of worsted yarn is part of his trade and he earns more than one shilling and sixpence each week and is not so poor as is alledged. When he gave up housekeeping, he sold his furniture but he is willing to give security on the administration as the Court shall determine.'

Both Kay and Lander replied to Livesy by confirming that the executors of Joseph Fourness were dead, as also were his daughters Martha, Mary, Ann and Lydia, but there was issue of Anne.

There was a grandchild living of Martha and Samuel Livesy, one of the administrators of the estate of Mary, the daughter and legatee named in the will of Joseph Fourness and the one surviving next of kin who had no interest in the residue of the Fourness estate. When Frances Fourness married Gabetis Norton she surrendered her title to Kay and Lander. Both admitted that neither Frances nor Gabetis, nor Kay or Lander were relatives of Joseph Fourness but they were well entitled to act as administrators of the estate of Joseph Fourness, now without administrators. The administration was duly transferred.[5]

12

TUTORS AND GUARDIANS

Occasionally a guardian would promote a cause in the court to retain the duty of guardian or tutor to a child when challenged by another party.

In 1722 Mary Walker, widow of Whitehaven, cited William Hodgson to show cause why the letters of tuition granted to him should not be revoked and granted to Mary Walker for the persons of John and Jane Thelkeld of Moresby. Mary Walker did not feel equal to the task and wrote:

> I do declare that contrary to my own inclination and desire was prevailed upon ... at the request of some of my relatives to issue this Citation ... I am in such a position of being incapable and in every way unfit to have the tuition of the said Infants granted me and incapacitated to discharge such a trust not being able to take care of myself, manage my own concerns and am very unwilling and averse to be anyway concerned either with the Education of the said Infants or management of their Estates.

Thomas Heslop and John Hudson saw the weakness of William Hodgson so they wrote the letter on behalf of Mary Walker and as a result they were appointed guardians.[1]

The case of John Fell is a similar one. When he died in 1725 he left a widow, Frances, and two sons, Christopher and John, who were both minors so the court appointed their mother as tutor. On 18 November 1725 Frances Fell made her will and left all her goods to Christopher Fell, her father-in-law, in trust for the use, 'benefit and advantage of the said minors and appointed Christopher Fell as executor and gave him forty shillings for his trouble and care relating to the said will'.

It appeared that Christopher Fell was indebted to his son the late John Fell in considerable amounts of money, which he had borrowed. This appeared in the accounts as a total of £283, a sum he had refused to pay John. Further it appeared that Christopher Fell's estate was mortgaged 'to one or more persons for one or more considerable sums of money on bond and that he is liable to be sued for debt'. It was considered that, under the circumstances, Christopher Fell was an 'improper person' to have the tutorship of any children and that James Rigmaiden was a far better person to have the administration of the estate and also the custody of the children in his hands.

On 6 July 1716, James Fenton, vicar of Lancaster and rural dean, stated that he knew nothing of any accounts, in the allegations against Christopher Fell, that concerned his son John Fell. However, he was convinced that Christopher Fell was indebted to several persons, including James Fenton himself. In fact, John Fell had given him a bond for £30, being part of the sum for the security of £80 mortgaged on the lands of Christopher Fell in Aughton. Though John had paid two years' interest on the money, Christopher was very dilatory in paying his just debts.

One witness, Robert Jepson, yeoman of Skerton, said that Christopher Fell owed his wife £10 and he was having a great deal of trouble in getting repayment of the debt. John Fell agreed to pay the £10 on his father's account. Further trouble was reported in that Christopher Fell, Daniel Heysham and Thomas Wilson had all borrowed jointly from his wife £15 on bond and Jepson had to take out a writ to recover the money. He was completely unaware how much money was owed to the others, but he himself was owed £30. Although Fell was not in straightened circumstances, Jepson considered that Rigmaiden would be a far better guardian.

James Holmes of Lancaster said that he was summoned on 18 November to draw up the will of Frances Fell. From the remarks made, he clearly understood that the wish of both John Fell and his wife was that the tuition of their children should go to Rigmaiden since Christopher Fell owed John the very large sum of £283.

Alexander Sherson of Lancaster confirmed that Fell's estate

was wholly mortgaged to one Oliver Marton and, since Christopher Fell 'is a notoriously bad payer of his debts, he is totally unfit to tutor children'. Hence the guardianship of the children went to Rigmaiden.[2]

A careless guardian could wreak havoc with the care and finances of an estate. In 1725 the Grosvenor family of Liverpool, in cooperation with William and Martha Mason, cited John Seacombe, the tutor of Robert Seacombe, into court for negligence. It appeared that Robert Seacombe senior, father to Martha and grandfather to Robert, who was a minor, left him a considerable amount of property:

    6 houses in Dale Street
    1 house in Castle Street
    6 parcels of land in Liverpool
    2 tenements in West Derby
    1 tenement in Cook Street
    22 houses in Cook Street

valued at £63. John Seacombe believed that the value of the property was no more than £44.18s.0d., and the rates, taxes and repairs amounted to £4.

The will was dated 2 September 1701, under which the testator, Robert Seacombe senior, bequeathed all his property to the use of Elizabeth Seacombe after the death of Ralph Seacombe, the father of Robert. The testator appointed Elizabeth and Ralph Seacombe, the latter having since died, as executors. Robert Seacombe's grandfather had died in Waterford, Ireland, and following his death Elizabeth left Ireland and came to live in Liverpool.

The Grosvenors, both Francis and Elizabeth, although they were closely related to the Seacombes, turned out to be a greedy and grasping family. They openly refused to let Elizabeth have any part of the estate save 'an iron pot'. John Seacombe was convinced that the Grosvenors took all the personal estate of the deceased which they proceeded to dispose of at their own will and pleasure, refusing to render any account at all to Elizabeth. William Mason, another relative of the Grosvenors, came especially to Liverpool to request that the personal estate of the deceased should be handed to him to take to the Grosvenors, but Elizabeth refused their request.

One of the problems arose from the fact that Ralph Seacombe, the son of Robert Seacombe, had issue of a son who, to confuse matters, was also named Robert, being the heir at law and an infant. Later Elizabeth Seacombe died and it had become impossible to trace any correspondence or papers that belonged to her. Everything of this nature had either been lost or more probably deliberately destroyed by the Grosvenors.

When Robert senior died, he owed £50 to Alderman James Dunn by bond and a further £10 to the Revd John Bolton, also secured by bond, plus several years accrued interest. And that was not all, for he owed a further £20 to Anne Foster of Dublin secured by bond with interest added.

It had cost Robert Seacombe so much money to make provision for his favourite daughters, Rebecca and Martha, that he died in much reduced circumstances. His estate consisted chiefly of houses and property in Liverpool which were in urgent need of repair. Since Elizabeth's death all the rents and profits had been spent on repairs to the property, with the inevitable result that there was insufficient money to clear the testator's debts.

It appeared that in her lifetime Elizabeth had received £16 from Robert, and the Grosvenors had satisfied themselves with a surplus from the estate. The Masons had received £15 from Elizabeth, but both the Grosvenors and the Masons wanted £100 each. Both parties requested that whatever they held in their hands from the estate should be set against their legacy. Overall the sum of £1,716 was disbursed in settling the estate and the debts, so that little Robert, the heir at law, was left with very little indeed to support him.[3]

The indifference shown by some tutors towards the children in their care – often involving child abuse, something not uncommon in the twentieth century – is well illustrated by a case from Bedale. William Kempe, a close relative of John Webster, brought an action against Richard Marsh for his treatment of William Webster. John Webster and his wife being dead, their two sons, John and William, were placed under the tuition of Thomas Thackwray and Richard Marsh. On the whole Thackwray appears to have been a good guardian and treated John Webster in a proper manner. Unfortunately it was otherwise for William. The allegations against Marsh were on the grounds that 'William Webster hath bene and yet is served by the wilfulness and negligence of Richard Marsh to go barefooted and bareheaded in rags and torn clothes, not sufficient to keep him warm'. Moreover, Marsh lived on Askew farm as guardian to William Webster and, during the time he was there, 'he did suffer the lease thereof, being the right and interest of the said William Webster in and to the same to be forfeited for non payment of the rents according to the said lease, and suffered the houses and buildings . . . to go to ruin and decay and the said Farm to be taken by another over the head of William Webster'.

William Kempe, who brought the case to court, proved beyond doubt that he was 'accounted to be the nearest blood relative' of William Webster and asked the court to grant him the tuition of William because Richard Marsh was no relative of the Websters in any way. The court granted his request and Richard Marsh was replaced as tutor by Kempe.[4]

Comparative wills from Gloucestershire follow a similar pattern. The will of Richard Adey of Sodbury deceased was contested at the request of Joan Adey against John and Thomas Adey, sons of Richard Adey, who died 21 May 1668. Also involved were Gertrude Booker and Elizabeth Philpot. This disputed will is one in which there are some complicated relationships.

In his will, Richard Adey named Thomas Adey and John Adey, his sons, as executors. When he found himself ill and weak, Richard sent his maidservant, Mary Rudley, to William Ellery to ask him to come over and write Richard's will. When Ellery returned home, he immediately went to see Richard Adey whom he found lying on his bed. Presently, Richard unlocked a chest from which he took out writing materials and two documents. The first paper was a lease and the second a bond which he asked Ellery to deliver to Thomas and John his executors, for Richard feared that his wife, being stepmother to Thomas and John Adey, might retain or embezzle them so that his will might not be fulfilled to his desire. The cause was heard on 6 October 1668.

The first witness was Ann Taylor, wife of Richard Taylor of Oldbury in Thornbury parish where she was born. She confirmed that Gertrude Booker had always been taken as the natural and lawful daughter of Richard Adey now deceased, who was taken by his mother (whose name she never knew), to be the brother to Edward Jackson senior, now dead. He was reputed to be the lawful father of Edward Jackson junior, also dead. She knew Edward Jackson very well and usually called him 'Uncle' since she was the daughter of Gertrude Booker, one of the parties involved in the dispute. Edward Jackson junior died intestate, as she had been reliably informed, without any issue and leaving behind him Elizabeth, his widow, who was now the wife of Philip Philpot. Edward Jackson at his death left neither 'father nor mother, brothers or sisters or any nephews and nieces' so far as she was aware. She had heard that Gertrude Booker and Edward Jackson were 'first cousins by half blood and she heard Edward Jackson confirm this'.

Responding to the questions put to her, Ann Taylor said that Gertrude Booker was her mother. Elizabeth Philpot she had known for thirty years and Richard Adey, a tailor by trade, was her grandfather. He had two wives during the course of his life. The first was Ann's grandmother, whose Christian name she could not remember. The second wife was one Joan, but she had no knowledge of her maiden name. She had also heard that Richard Adey had three children, Richard, who died as a child, Gertrude and Mary, who 'went beyond the seas about thirty years ago and was never more since heard of'.

By his second wife Richard Adey had a daughter named Elizabeth, who married William Whitfield by whom she had a child now living named William Whitfield. Ann believed that her grandfather was about 50 years old when he died, and that was forty years previously. Ann also knew Edward Jackson senior, the father of Edward Jackson, but it was more than thirty years since he had died. She had heard her mother say that Edward Jackson senior was the son of Elizabeth, mother of Richard Adey. The only persons entitled to a share of the contested estate were Gertrude Booker and Edward Jackson's widow, now the wife of Philip Philpot, but she was in no way related to the litigants. Ann Taylor admitted that she was the daughter of Gertrude Booker and she would 'gain the victory in this cause if it lay in her power to get it'. Ann was convinced that she had a right to a dividend from Edward Jackson's estate.

Guy Lawrence, vicar of Thornbury, was called next. He admitted that he knew both Richard Adey and Edward Jackson senior, the father of Edward Jackson deceased, 'concerning whose personal estate' was now in dispute before the court. Both Richard Adey and Edward Jackson were reputed to be brothers by half blood, but whether by their mother Elizabeth he did not know.

From the age of 4 or 5 years he well remembered Gertrude, now the wife of Nicholas Booker, living with Richard and Joan Adey, whose Dame school Lawrence attended. Richard Adey did own that Gertrude was his lawful daughter:

> as such she was admitted to a customary estate within the Manor of Thornbury after the death of Richard Adey and Joan his second wife and the forfeiture of the second husband of Joan Adey deceased of the yearly value of above seventy pounds per Annum by the homage & Stewards of the said Manor which she enjoyed as a Coppyhold of Inheritance. She has since sold or surrendered the said estate to several persons reserving to herself some annuity of the same for her life.

When Edward Jackson died he had no close relatives still alive, but Lawrence heard that Edward Jackson senior married the widow of one Pruett of Oldbury by whom he had a son, also Edward. Joan had by her first husband two sons, who both had children living. Also Edward Jackson and Gertrude Booker were 'first Cozens by halfe blood', but whether by Elizabeth he did not know. Replying to the questions put to him at the hearing, Guy Lawrence stated that he had known Gertrude Booker for fifty years, Elizabeth Jackson for thirty and Richard Adey for as many years as he could recollect.

Then he provided a clue to the surname of Richard Adey's second wife before her marriage, when she was Joan Stone. Richard had two daughters, Gertrude and Mary, by his first wife, and one daughter, Elizabeth, by his second wife, who married William Whitfield. Nothing had been heard of Mary for more than forty years.

Joan Pruett had, before her marriage to Richard Adey, four children, Thomas, John, Elizabeth and Mary. The eldest, John, lived at Oldbury upon Severn and Elizabeth was the wife of Joseph Neal of Oldbury. Thomas and Mary were now dead. Thomas Pruett left two sons, Thomas and John, who both lived at Cowhill in Thornbury, and a daughter Eleanor, the widow of Ralph Cooke, who also resided in Cowhill. He considered that John Pruett ought to be entitled to a share of the estate of Edward Jackson, as should Gertrude Booker.

A third witness was Richard Harwood, fisherman of Thornbury, who had known the parties for thirty years and the late Richard Adey for over forty years. Richard had married Joan Pruett for his second wife and he was able to confirm the relationship between Gertrude Booker and Elizabeth Philpot. He knew Edward Jackson, father of Edward deceased, and that Edward Jackson was the son of Elizabeth, the mother of Richard Adey, but he was unable to verify the veracity of the statement. The only ones who were entitled to a share of the estate were Gertrude Booker and Elizabeth Philpot.

One witness, Thomas Barrow of Oldbury, said that Gertrude Booker was the lawful daughter of Richard Adey, who was 'brother by halfe blood' to Edward Jackson senior. He was taken to be the lawful father of Edward Jackson deceased, whose estate was the subject of the current dispute. Gertrude Booker now enjoyed a copyhold estate in Thornbury as the heiress at law of Richard Adey, but he did not know if Richard Adey was the lawful brother by his mother to Edward Jackson.

Edward Jackson junior died intestate, leaving a daughter Elizabeth as his heiress, who was now the wife of Philip Philpot. Barrow affirmed that Gertrude Booker and Edward Jackson were always assumed to be 'first cousins' by 'halfe blood'. Richard Adey and Edward Jackson called each other 'brother'; he had heard them use that term when he had been in their company, and they were taken for such by their neighbours. Gertrude and Elizabeth shared the estate.[5]

13

NON COMPOS MENTIS

Ambitious relatives and friends who were unwilling to risk the opportunity to inherit or benefit by a will could feel very threatened by the attitude and actions of the testator. So they could and did try, sometimes in vain, to provide proof that the testator was not in his correct mind and had been open to influence by others.

John Charnley of Grimsargh had appointed Roger Charnock as his executor, who was challenged by Elizabeth Cavannaugh that he had exerted influence on Charnley in making his will. One witness, Thomas Whittaker, confirmed that he was present with the deceased on 2 February 1737 together with John Werdon. Whittaker was very disatisfied with some persons who were present with the testator and turning to John Werden he said: 'Damn them, what business had anyone to meddle for they have ordered it just as they had a mind to.' Whittaker was an apprentice and articled to Charnley, so he expected to be a beneficiary under the will.

Further questioning revealed that, on 12 June 1736, Whittaker found his master insensible and in no fit state to make a will. In fact he was so indisposed that he would reply 'Yes' to any question he was asked.

Whittaker then stated that if he could be indemnified from his articles of indenture he would be able to express himself freely upon the will and the pressures put upon him when Charnley was making his will. Isabel Charnley, his widow, replied that John her husband had been very ill and extremely indisposed for a long time. For several days before his death, he was not sensible and in no fit condition to make his will. For three days before his death, he was unable to recognize his close friends and relatives and his condition deteriorated so quickly that he died on 9 February 1737.

Charnley had made two wills, but for several days his understanding was so bad that he could not read over the wills, neither were they read to him. In this condition he was unable to make a clear disposition of his estate, which amounted to some £7,000. The court found that John Charnley had drawn a will without due consideration for the welfare of his wife and family. Since John Werden would inherit the property without the widow and his children having provision made for them as the law required; the will was declared null and void. Holding an estate of that value encouraged his friends and relatives to behave like vultures over a dead carcase.[1]

An attempt in 1730 to declare that William Craig, mariner of Whitehaven, was *non compos mentis* was foiled in the end. On 25 August 1730, Robert Dixon, Jane Dixon, Robert Gilpin and Hannah Craig, their infant sister, wanted the will declared null and void because of the manner in which the deceased disposed of his shipping interests.

It was the custom for small trading ships to be constructed with a number of people (as many as twenty) each holding a share in the vessel and drawing a share of the profits.[2] In this case William Craig had disposed of his interests outside his relatives and they were prepared to argue that he had no right to do this against their interests. So the four opponents decided to challenge the authority of John Monk, the executor.

The opponents stated that the infant sister, Hannah Craig, was half sister on her father's side to William Craig and the nearest in kin to William at the time of his death who at that time was incapable of making a will.

George Atkinson, merchant of Whitehaven, said Craig was very much indisposed when he asked him to draw his will. At that time, Atkinson, being a single man, was lodging with the same family as Craig. The testator appointed his friend, John Monk, as executor and the will was read over in the presence of Martha Williamson, Anne Gregson and the testator.

Robert Dixon confirmed that he had known the testator for many years and that he was a distant relative. In his opinion the deceased was quite capable of making a will and no malpractice had been used to influence him. He denied that he had said that

Craig had no right to dispose of the shipping in his will, for that was a limited interest.

The will was drawn up in the house of Mercy Atkinson between 'two in the afternoon and midnight', with the testator sitting upon his bed, where he executed the same in the presence of witnesses and the executor's wife, Mary Monk.

The will was then handed to Martha Williamson, who was a widow and lived with her sister Mercy Atkinson where Craig had lodged for the past six years. George Atkinson, who also lodged with Mercy Atkinson, agreed to draw the will, which was then read over aloud. Martha also stated that Robert Dixon was second cousin to the deceased and although Craig was sensible on the day he made his will, yet the following day he was 'disordered in his head'. She had never heard Craig question his right to dispose of his shipping interest, for no such will and codicil would have been written. The court decreed that Craig was *non compos mentis* and the will was declared null and void.[3]

On 21 June 1684, the will of Gyles Harding, tailor, of Cirencester was contested by his relatives on the grounds that he was not in possession of his faculties at the time. In his will he had left 10s. to each of the children of John Spark, 40s. to the children of his cousins Hester Painter and Mary Carter, with the residue of the estate to his cousin Gyles Harding, who was also the executor. The dispute was between the two relatives Spark and Harding.

The first witness was Mary Ashmead of Cirencester, who said she was born in Crudwell in Wiltshire but had been resident in Cirencester for the last two years. On 21 June 1683 she went to visit Gyles Harding, at which time he asked her whose horse won the race on the Downs, by which she believed he meant Cerney Downs. She told him there was no horse racing at the time, to which remark he replied 'there was and my Lord's horse won the race'. This remark made her believe that he was not of sound mind and memory, for there was no racing on the Downs at that time.

John Painter of Cirencester, yeoman, said that he went to visit Gyles Harding then very ill at his house. Enquiring about his health, Harding said that 'he was pretty well', which he doubted for the deceased appeared to be 'decomposed in his intellect'. This was even more marked when John Pitman came to see him and solicited him to make his will. Whereupon Harding replied, '"Noe" for he intended to have a wife with a great deal of money . . . which expression did not argue the sanity of his mind considering the grievous distemper and sickness he then laboured under'.

Judith Spark of Cirencester, widow aged 70, said she had been born in Bisley but had lived in Cirencester for fifty years. She also stated that Gyles Harding, the executor, had told her that the deceased had left 40s to John Painter and his children, 40s. to John Carter and his children, 40s. to John Spark and his children, and 40s. to John Firkett, but that she had received 'not one farthing'.

Mary Spencer, hearing of the illness of Harding, decided to pay him a visit and attempt to recover a debt of £6 from him. She said she was the wife of William Spencer and had lived in Cirencester for twenty years, having been born in Latton in Wiltshire. She went to see Harding to demand the £6 she had lent to Harding's wife, who was also dead. Upon her arrival, she found Gyles Harding's wife sitting with the sick man. Finding the old man very much indisposed, she told Harding's wife what she had come for. Harding's wife then gave her this sharp reply: 'Pray let him alone for he has not been sensible this two or three days.' Mary Spencer's reaction was to leave immediately without her £6.

Margaret Symms said that she had been born in Farington in Berkshire forty-six years ago and had lived in Cirencester for seventeen years. When she went to visit Harding, Gyles Harding came into the room where his uncle lay, and with him were Ralph Willet, Mr Small and John Webb. Harding then informed his uncle that he had brought three honest men with him so that he could make his will. Harding then replied:

he could not do it neither would he, but he was told that it is a thing that must be done if you can. He then turned his head from them towards the wall and played with a napkin which lay upon the bedd, foulding the same into the shape of a Child's baby and admiring the same which was a great instance of his insanity of mind.

When Harding was in complete possession of his faculties, Thomas Burgo, a tailor of Cirencester, frequently visited him. Even during his final sickness, Burgo continued to call upon him but found him 'discomposed in mind and memoray'. On one occasion he found Harding busy pulling down a vine that grew up the side of his house. Another time he found Harding getting out of bed and 'Putting on his breeches over his Arms instead of his Coate and saying that he would go with him to the house of Arthur Little to drink Ale and help John Painter to make hay'.

The court found that the deceased was totally incapable of making any will and appointed an administrator.[4]

The two sons of Thomas Collier of Stonehouse, who died in 1712, quarrelled over their father's will. Thomas accused his brother Stephen of forging the will. Stephen alleged that his father never signed his will, nor did he publish it, but that his brother Thomas put a pen into his father's hand and wrote the name Thomas Collier 'as it now appears in the will' and he directed how the will should be drawn up.

Thomas Collier senior had told several persons that he had made a will and, furthermore, 'he had kept his Children quiet in his lifetime and would endeavour to keep them so after his decease'. He had bequeathed a cupboard to his son Stephen, implying by this action that the estate was not charged with any money, although the will charged Stephen Collier with the payment of several sums of money left as legacies.

His son Thomas said that his father's illness was so serious that he was not *compos mentis* and showed no interest whatever in his will. He continued by stating that his brother Stephen took advantage of his father's condition and contrived with William Jackson and William Parslow to make his will for him. His father was totally incapable of making a will or knowing what it was about or what it contained.

John Hilton, vicar of Stonehouse, called on 29 May 1712 to see Thomas Collier, 'who was very ill of the Small Pox and prayed with him but noticed no disorder in his mind'.

Jane Harmer of Stonehouse visited Collier on 30 May and found William Parslow with him. During some conversation Collier told her that he did 'Pretty easy and hoped he should doe well if he could stop the Flux . . . he said that he had a sore throat and asked for some Dogstard and Honey, requesting Jane to ask his Nurse for some. The nurse replied, "What so near he be for death".' Collier also told her that Mrs Nash, a neighbour, was a very good neighbour who had done a great deal of good work in the parish and she believed that he was of sound mind and memory.

Jonathon David of Stonehouse was not present when the will was written but he believed that the testator was sensible, 'although sick with the small pox'. He saw William Parslow give a pen to Thomas Collier's son, who placed it in the testator's hand. Thomas Collier senior then scribbled a mark on the paper. When questioned about this, David declared that he was unable to recall the gestures the testator made or if he sealed his will without the aid of his son Thomas.

Samuel Wellcose, the joiner, said that he went to see Collier on 29 May in the late evening, but was summoned by Parslow next day to go with him to see Collier. On arriving, he found Jonathon Davies present and Collier's two sons were drawing details of their father's debts. Both Wellclose and Parslow were asked to withdraw; when they were recalled they were shown the will and asked to witness it. Both believed that the testator was of sound mind. When William Parslow, the blacksmith, went to Collier's on 30 May, at his request in order to draw his will, it was an old will naming Collier's wife as executor, but she had been dead many years.

When he was asked to name his executor, Collier replied 'Tom', meaning his son Thomas. Collier then said that if his daughter Mary, then lying ill, should die, her sister Ursula should only have her legacy. He ordered that his cottage should be shared between Thomas and Ursula and they should pay 3s. each as a token. Also he would pay out of his house 'and backside forty pounds to pay his debts but he would do nothing more for Stephen'.

Stephen Collier is typical of the jealous brother who aims to get as much of the estate as he is able to. Sadly, this is an attitude that is found at the present time.[5]

14

NUNCUPATIVE WILLS

Nuncupative wills are wills that were spoken orally and later committed to writing. They were very common, doubtless because many people were reluctant to make a will, believing that to do so brought death closer, so the decision was delayed until it was almost too late. Failure to find someone capable of drawing a will or the onset of a fatal disease meant that the will had to be spoken orally to witnesses standing round, whose duty it was to remember what the testator said and later to write down the details and ask for probate.

In 1699, Peter Rogerson of Little Budworth in Cheshire made a nuncupative will which led to a dispute between Catherine Rogerson, his widow, and Henry Briscall, his executor. On 3 January 1699, Peter Rogerson was taken seriously ill, an illness from which he was never to recover. He decided to call in a neighbour, John Billington, a farmer of Little Budworth, to come and draw up his will. Being late in the day, Billington decided, with typical rural equanimity, that the next day would be as convenient to draw the will as the present one.

So when he called at Rogerson's house the following day, he found Rogerson 'sitting on a Couch in the dwelling place of his house when he disposed of his estate in all things and he said the schedule should stand for his will'. John Walker, a witness from Little Budworth, said that Rogerson wanted Henry Briscall and John Billington to be joint executors, but Billington refused because 'a certain person who had a debt of five pounds owing the deceased, would probably be sued in Court and this person was a friend of Billington'. In other words, loyalty to one's friends takes precedence when acting as an executor. Catherine Rogerson wanted the will annulled on the grounds that her late husband had made too little provision for her future welfare and she faced insecurity. The will was annulled.[1]

Alice Frith, a spinster from Sandy Lane in Audlem, declared her nuncupative will in 1660, but her brother, Richard Frith, contested the will against the executors, Thomas Sutton and Jonathon Scills. Dorothy Sutton, Alice Frith's sister, said that Alice had declared her mind and will, saying that, when all the funeral costs and her debts had been paid, then all her goods should go to Dorothy Frith, the youngest daughter of Richard Frith, and this should include two heifers.

Then followed evidence of a very common practice designed to avoid the expense of collecting a debt from a friend or relative. Alice left Richard Frith's son Richard 'two pounds of a debt that he owed her' as well as 10s., being the sum he might expect from the estate.

To Mary Frith Alice left the 'greatest brass pot and a pair of linen sheets'. Two of Richard's sons, namely Thomas and William, were to receive 20s. each and sufficient linen cloth to make Thomas two shirts. To Thomas she also bequeathed the table and frame on which it stood, which at the time of her death was in the part of the house then occupied by William Bate. Ellen and Gabriel Frith, another son and daughter, were to have 20s. divided between them. Margaret, the wife of Thomas Ravenshaw of Malpas, was left a looking glass and one napkin, while Martha Robinson, her neighbour, was to have one linen apron.

The chief beneficiary was her niece Dorothy Sutton, for the estate was to be used for the preferment of Dorothy and her sister Ellen, with the major part going to Dorothy. However, a day or two before she died Alice decided to change her nuncupative will and said 'I give all my goods which I die possessed of to Richard Frith's children only and I would have his younger daughter to be a little better considered than the rest'.[2]

Another nuncupative will was that of Thomas Benson, yeoman of Claughton, which was made in Garstang market in 1723. It was said that at the time of making his will Benson was weak and infirm in body and 'sick of the last sickness of which he died'. He evidently had lived almost the whole of his life in the house in which he died, as indeed many people did at that time.

John Gorse, yeoman of Claughton, stated that he had spoken with Benson in Garstang market on Thursday 9 January, when Benson told him that he would give him £3 to be added to the 40s. which Gorse owed to Benson, 'which money he intended to pay for his funeral'. When Gorse asked what should be done with the rest of his effects, he replied that they should go to William Gurnell. Since there were no other witnesses present in the market, Benson gave strict instructions to Gorse that he should remember what words had been spoken. Gorse never saw Benson again, for he died ten days later. Gurnell was very curious to discover what Benson had left, so he decided to see Gorse in Garstang market on the Thursday after Benson's funeral and ask him what he remembered about Benson's will. Gorse gave him the same reply as he had given in his evidence, that the £5 should be used to pay for his funeral and the remainder should go to Gurnell.

Margaret Ireland, aged 69, stated that on Wednesday 19 January, 'soon after he had got out of bed' she decided that she should send for her daughter Mary Johnson, being most concerned because Benson was so very feeble and she 'would have him make his will'. Replying to a question on the matter, Benson had stated that William Gurnell should have all he had in goods (perhaps £1,000) except £5, 'to bring him home handsomely in some style' to be buried. Both witnesses confirmed that the words were spoken in their presence.

It was evident that both women had from time to time encouraged Benson to make his will in writing, 'which would make peace', but all Benson would say in reply was: 'do you take notice of my words – it will be will enough.'

Mary Johnson, aged 40, said that she was sent for 'when he [Benson] was very feeble' and her mother thought that he would not live long. Benson then informed her, in the presence of William Gurnell, who was there at the time, that Gurnell should have all he had if it was £1,000, except for what would bury him, for Gurnell had shown him 'very great kindness'. She then confirmed that the words Benson had spoken were written down by Mr Garner in his house in Garstang, in the presence of John Gorse and herself. As Benson appeared to have no relatives, a general citation was issued for any interested persons to appear at the proving of the will. One distant relative appeared, Robert Chippindale, a linen weaver from Claughton, but he raised no objections.[3]

A considerable number of contested wills concern small craftsmen, so it is by no means surprising to find a will of a bricklayer, John Bayley of Preston, who had died on 16 April 1723. After he had spoken his will orally, he gave some very good reasons why he was leaving all to his daughters and nothing to his son, for the latter was a spendthrift and his daughters very caring and loving. His spoken will was committed to writing six days later.

Alice Edleston, his daughter and wife of John Edleston, was the principal legatee in his nuncupative will and inventory. The value of the estate came to a total of £12.18s.0d. Alice said that her father, at his death, had the lease of the dwelling house for a number of years, but the value of his estate was in reality worth no more than stated.

John Sanderson, an innkeeper of Preston, maintained that Bayley was of sound mind and memory when he declared his will. One of Edleston's daughters called for his wife, Mary, to come and see her father Bayley. Bayley told her when he saw her that she was to take careful note of the words he spoke. Sanderson subscribed his name as a witness when the spoken words were written down, but he did not believe Bayley's effects were worth £20, which Edleston claimed that they were. Indeed, it was clear that Edleston's ambition was to obtain the entire estate as Bayley's son-in-law, having married Mary Bayley.

Bayley had permitted his son-in-law Edleston to share part of his house for living quarters. Robert Brook, linen weaver of Preston, stated that Bayley 'Gave that part of the house in which John Edleston lived with a Barn and Fould belonging and the further part of the Garden to his daughter Alice during the remaining term of the Lease'. Bayley also desired that his daughters Alice and Mary should have 'The other part of the house and nearer side of the Garden betwixt them during the Term of the Lease'.

Edleston then sent for Brook to be a witness to the spoken words and confirm that those in the written will were identical. Samuel Peploe, vicar of Preston and rural dean, before whom the will had to be proved (being less than £40 in value), became suspicious. He made enquiries and amended the citation issued for interested parties to appear to read as follows:

I likewise certify that there is no such person as John Eccleston [Edleston] that I know of & that the person intended is as I suppose a very honest but extremely poor man & ready at any time to do what is fit to be done without any proceedings against him.

By this statement Peploe implied that poor men were entirely unreliable as witnesses because they were open to bribery and undue influence. As a result, Edleston lost his claim to the estate, which was shared between the two daughters, Alice and Mary, as the testator desired.[4]

Quite often a will reveals the love and affection, or otherwise, that existed between a testator and his wife during their lifetime.

One example is the nuncupative will of Edmund Jones of Hengengates in Middleton, which was contested by his widow, Alice, against John and Henry Jones, his two sons. Clearly Edmund Jones intended that his children were to benefit from his estate:

That John and Henry my cozens by Blood shall have two parts of my goods viz. my own part and the third part which I have reserved and given to my Children. . . . It is my will and mind that my wyffe shall never have anything to do with any part of the goods which I have or are due unto my Children but that John and Henry shall have usage and disposition of the said goods for the benefit of his child or Children until she or they attain the years of Full Age and Discretion.[5]

The will was upheld as valid and his poor wife got nothing.

On 12 December 1736 Austin Chadwick of Chadderton, a millwright, dictated his will in the house in which he had lived for the previous twenty years, in the presence of six witnesses. Austin, unlike so many other testators, made provision for his wife, Mary, so that after his death she would have somewhere to live and also a small income to support her. Moreover, Mary was to have the use of the kitchen for the duration of her life, 'being part of the messuage in which he lived'. In addition, she was to have two closes called Blackheath with standing for two cows and pay 10s. a year to his son, Daniel, as a rent.

This enterprising millwright also owned or held shares in

some coal mines, for the mining industry was beginning to expand in that part of Lancashire. He declared that the 'remainder of the estate with the profits from the coal mynes to his six youngest children and his wife Mary to be divided equally between them and to share and share alike'. Such a sentiment is typical of parts of the north at this time where families stuck closely together in the new mining communities.

The remainder of the message and the parlour were to be used by Mary during her lifetime, it being the custom to make good provision for one's widow. After Mary's death the remainder of the message was to revert to his son Daniel.[6] The will was duly accepted for probate.

The presence of friends and relatives crowding round the bed in which a testator lay dying could and did lead to confusion. When Roger Laithwayt of Westhoughton died in 1661, his widow, Jane, was utterly confused as to what her late husband had really decided to do with his estate.

John Hindley and John Laithwayt alias Halliwell were the executors who had to reply to Jane Laithwayt's allegations. According to Jane, her late husband made a will, which she said was nuncupative, on 9 August 1661. In his will he made certain bequests:

> to Elizabeth Weatherbie the sum of forty shillings, to John Laithwayt ten shillings and to his daughter twenty shillings and the rest of the estate to his widow Jane Laithwayt. This was uttered and declared before Jane Laithwayt, James Watmough and Elizabeth Roome.

Replying to the questions put to her, Jane said that her husband died about the time stated and made a will, but whether the will shown to her was 'her husband's' or not 'she does not know'. It was her belief that on 27 October, the day on which he died, there were too many friends with and about him, like so many vultures wanting to discover if he had made a will.

Jane Laithwayt in like manner was filled with curiosity and, being anxious to discover what the real situation was, took John Laithwayt alias Halliwell, being one of the executors, out of the room into the back porch and asked him directly to tell her if he had any wills or writings in his possession, but he denied all knowledge of anything. She then pressed him to visit his uncle and satisfy himself about these matters, but he stubbornly refused, like a good executor.

Jane Laithwayt said that between 10 and 11 in the morning of 27 October her husband declared his wishes, which were written down in the nuncupative will which Jane exhibited in court personally and the will had been witnessed by James Watmough and Elizabeth Roome. The executors confirmed that Roger Laithwayt was dead and Jane his wife, but now his widow, who 'is commonly taken to be so' by her neighbours. The will was accepted and probate granted.[7]

John Welsh blacksmith of Ince, Wigan, who died on 12 February 1661, made a nuncupative will by which he appointed his two sons, Robert and Fletcher Welsh, as his executors. The will was contested by his daughter, Margaret Griffiths, who considered that she had received too little from the estate and that her father was of unsound mind. Thomas Hale, yeoman of Ince, said that on 27 December 1660, a short time before Welsh died, he paid Welsh a visit and found him to be unwell. Welsh said that 'he had a desire to make his will . . . and did declare his mind on all points contained in the schedule'. Thomas Hale then wrote down what Welsh declared and he read it over to John Welsh, Elizabeth Clough and Robert and Fletcher Welsh, who were witnesses. During the whole of the time the will was being noted, the testator appeared to be in full possession of his faculties.

Elizabeth Clough, a widow of Ince, said that at the time the will was spoken she was with Thomas Hale, sitting with John Welsh, who, like many elderly parents, lived with one of the sons, Robert Welsh, in his house. She affirmed that the will was as written in the schedule. The value of the deceased's estate was £34.15s.0d., out of which was paid £6 for the funeral, and he bequeathed the following:

to Ellen and Robert Clough the remainder of four pounds for their use being eighteen shillings
to Robert Welsh money from the deceased's clothes and other necessaries – ten shillings
to Mary Thornley his niece charges for certain tools – ten shillings
to Ellen Adamson for shirt cloth – two shillings.

The will was finally proved and Margaret Griffiths lost her case.[8]

The will of William Garner, farmer of Urswick, in 1729 could have been the source of a contest. Garner had originally intended to appoint James Mount and Leonard Park as his executors, but between July and September he changed his mind and replaced Leonard Park with Henry Park. His trustees were to have £5 for their trouble. He decided finally that Christopher Cowper should be his sole executor.

On 10 October the testator was taken seriously ill. He died on the 23rd of the same month and was never in a position to execute the will. However, since all his legacies were to be given to relatives and 'kindred', the will as drawn by William Park of Ulverston was declared to be a valid one. There was one flaw, in that Christopher Cowper was a minor and could not legally act as an executor, so that duty went to Henry Park.[9]

The nuncupative will of Jane Eastham of Walton le Dale was contested by John Eastham against Henry Eastham, her brother, and Elizabeth Thornton. Since the testator was weak in body she made her will on 14 July 1664 in words and no writing. She declared that the costs of her funeral were to come out of her goods and she bequeathed the following legacies:

> To her nephew George Eastham she gave twenty pounds he being the son of her brother Robert Eastham.
>
> To John Eastham son of Robert, a Cover which Margaret Hawkshead of Walton had of her.
>
> To Margaret Sheridan daughter of her sister Alice Curedon, twenty shillings.
>
> To Elizabeth Eastham and Jane Eastham the daughters of her brother Robert Eastham, all her linen clothes.
>
> To her brother Henry Eastham the residue and remainder of her estate.

She appointed Henry Eastham as sole executor in the presence of several witnesses.

As in so many cases of contested wills, there was one very aggrieved and disappointed relative, John Eastham was most resentful because he had been omitted from Jane's will, while the rest of her relatives had all benefited. In the end he failed in his attempt to get the will overthrown.[10]

Attempts to claim a closer relationship to the deceased than existed arose in the case of the will of Elizabeth Hunt of Oldham. When she made her nuncupative will, Elizabeth named John

Taylor as her executor. However, the guardians of Elizabeth Taylor of Ashton under Lyne challenged the right of John Taylor to act as executor. After all, Elizabeth Hunt had spoken her will orally and had not had it written down.

First, she commended her soule unto Almightie God.

Item, it was her mind and will that her bodie should be buried in her father's pew within the Church or Chappell of Oldham.

Item she did give to the poore who came to her burial one pence apiece.

Item she did give and bequeath unto Katherine Taylor twentie pounds

Item she did give and bequeath unto Elizabeth Taylor one hundred pounds if she had it, or that her goods would reach or extend so far.

John Cowper, Rafe Tetlow and Edward Taylor were all present when she declared her will.

The three witnesses when the will was declared stated that Elizabeth Taylor was, in their view, the nearest living relative of Elizabeth Hunt. Indeed, there was said to be 'a common voice and fame' in Oldham that Elizabeth Taylor, though a minor, was closer in relationship to the deceased than was John Taylor. They also thought that the administration should have been granted to Elizabeth Taylor and James Holden jointly, and that Taylor should have costs awarded against him.

The appearance at the time when the will was ready to be proved of another but closer relative could and did lead to a great deal of expense. In the end, John Taylor was sentenced in costs for his temerity in claiming a close relationship with the deceased.[11]

When Daniel Gardner of Gloucester died, his brother, Thomas Gardner, challenged Daniel's widow, Rebecca, about the administration of his brother's estate, which he thought should have been his duty by right.

Richard Cowcher of the parish of St Catherine, Gloucester, said that about the 'fourth or fifth day of May last he went to visit the deceased, then lying ill'. When he arrived at the house, he found Thomas Iles sitting with him and when Iles asked Daniel if he would 'settle his mind' and give anything to his relatives, Gardner stated that 'he had nothing to dispose of from the old woman [meaning his wife] and what he had was little enough for her'. These words, which were spoken in the presence of Richard Cowcher, Thomas Iles and Charles Greenway, he intended should stand as his nuncupative will. All stated that he was 'of perfect memory' and, before Iles entered the room, he had said that he would give 'his old Freize Coat' to Walter Greenway, one of his journeymen. Daniel Gardner had no confidence whatsoever in the honesty of his brother Thomas who, if he got the opportunity, would wrong Rebecca and alienate her rights in his own interest. Daniel preferred Iles to act as administrator in place of Thomas and the court agreed.[12]

The will of Jane Cull of Yarmsworth, who died in 1684, was contested by John Cull, May Young and Anna Mace, the wife of Charles Mace, who believed she was of unsound mind. Anna Mace had attended Jane in her last illness and had cared for her. On 16 August 1684, in her brother Guy Cull's house in Yamsworth, the deceased, in the presence of Anna Mace, Giles Lawrence and Charles Mace, spoke her will. Although she was very sick, yet 'she wished that right may prevail'. As is customary in the diocese of Gloucester, the witnesses had not only to give their ages but the length of time they had resided in the parish. Giles Laurence of Yamsworth said that he had lived in Yamsworth for thirty-four years, having been born at Aldesworth, and was now 56 years old. He said that, on 16 August 1684, he came to the house, being a near neighbour to Guy Cull, who informed him that his sister Jane Cull lay very sick at his 'said party agents house' and she wanted to make her will. Guy asked him to be a witness. When he arrived he found Jane Cull very sick but of a sound mind in her brother's house.

Charles Mace said he had lived at Yamsworth for nine months, having been born in Winchcombe, and was 17 years of age. He said that he served Guy Cull and had been a hired servant for nine months. After Jane Cull's death he then lived as a 'sojourner'. He clearly remembered the words of the will being spoken on 16 August 1684 at the time of her last sickness.[13]

George Beamond of Stoak, who died in 1661, had declared his nuncupative will on 7 February 1659 'by word of mouth'. He had his tenement in Stoak on a lease during the lives of Bridget Moreton and Ellenor Meacocke from Sir Henry Bunbury of Stanney, one of the local gentry in the district. The remainder of the lease he bequeathed to his sister Alice, the wife of Thomas Johnson.

Henry Lightfoot of Stoak, a yeoman aged 31, said that a day or two before he died George Beamond did declare his will in his presence and also that of William Sephton and Midget Moreton.[14]

When Thomas Johnson of Kelton in Romaldkirk parish died in 1687 his will was contested by Isabella, the wife of William Ewbank, a blood relation of the deceased, and Christopher Bailes of Kelton, who had married Johnson's daughter. William Ewbank said that on 10 August 1686 at about 10 in the morning when he was leaving his house in Kelton, he saw Thomas Johnson standing at Christopher Bailes' door. He, being very intimate with and a little related to Thomas Johnson, went over to ask him how he did. Johnson replied that he was in 'indifferent good health and better than he had been formerly'. Johnson also told him what substance he had given to Christopher Bailes and that he did 'intend to live and remain with him'. Thomas Johnson, who was of perfect mind and memory, lived about a year after this meeting with Christopher Bailes, his son-in-law. He heard Johnson say that he had a very great kindness and respect for Christopher Bailes.

Another witness, William Bailes of Gill House, Balderdaile, a yeoman aged 66, said he was with Johnson a year before he died and discussing the disposal of his estate with him in Christopher Bailes' house. Johnson told him that he would give Christopher Bailes all he had, except 20s. towards the building of a stone bridge near Kelton. Bequests in wills for the repair or building of stone bridges still lingered in this part of the country.

Bailes went on to say that Johnson had considered making Christopher Bailes a deed of gift of all that he possessed. This witness advised him not to be so rash, for 'he would have him keep what he had knowing not how long he might live and what he might stand in need of himself'. Bailes said that, at the time Johnson was speaking or declaring his will, he was of perfect mind and memory, being none by or present except Thomas Johnson and himself. Probate was granted to Bailes.[15]

In April 1729, John Hartley of Browe in Eskdale, a farmer aged 36, said he was summoned from his bed, he having retired for the night, by John Wilson, nephew to Isabel Tyson, to come and act as a witness to her will. He arose from his bed and went with Wilson to his aunt's house. When he arrived, there he was led into the room where she lay in bed. He asked her how she did, to which she replied 'she was very ill and had a mind to dispose of her Effects'. He replied that there was no harm in that. She then proceeded to declare her mind and to dispose of her effects as in the writing annexed, making her sister, Susan, an executrix.

John Wilson of Gilbank and Mary Tyson of Bool in Eskdale were present with the witness when she declared her will. She lived for twenty-four hours longer and was of perfect mind and memory 'as she spoke the words of her will and the witnesses promised that they would do as she requested and put the testamentary words into writing the day Isabel was interred and immediately after her Buryall'.

The witnesses subscribed their names or marks on the day of the interment, which they thought was 22 April 1729. The will was accepted.[16]

The will of Richard Arrowsmith of Preston, yeoman, gives the impression of some very suspicious dealings. The will was contested by Alice Arrowsmith, widow, now the wife of Thomas Parkinson, against James Sittgreaves and Richard Duckworth, executors. The chief witness was John Green, a yeoman aged 52 years. He said that Arrowsmith came to visit him on the previous 11 April to ask him to draw up his will, which he did according to the directions given by the testator. He stated that the document shown to him was the will he drew up on 11 April 1728, which was duly signed, witnessed and sealed by himself and Dorothy Green.

Green had asked the testator if it was his will that James Sittgreaves and Richard Duckworth should have the remainder of the estate for their use after his debts, legacies and funeral expenses had been paid, in case Arrowsmith's son, John, a sickly boy, should die before he attained full age and unmarried. The testator replied 'No'; he intended the same for the good and relief of the Poor and such as stood in need, but gave no names of particular persons or places. It was intended that Green should come to the testator's dwelling house at some convenient time to advise him how to settle what was bequeathed to James Sittgreaves and Richard Duckworth.

This witness, 'being a labouring man', neglected to do so, despite a request to him to meet the testator at Preston fair, held the previous August, at which he never appeared. The document alleged to be a codicil to the testator's will, dated 11 October 1728 and signed by John Green, was written by him the day following the death of the testator according to the wish of the testator and information from other persons and as an explanation of the testator's will and not otherwise. He thought that he was obliged to do this to make good his neglect of not declaring the testator's will afresh during the deceased's lifetime as he was desired.

When questioned by Sittgreave and Duckworth, Green replied that he had not written the codicil until after the death of the testator, which he did as an explanation of the testator's will as he thought he was obliged to do. Further, the codicil was written at his house in Wittingham on the Sunday preceding Michaelmas day last, in the chamber over the parlour, and there were no persons present to whom he could refer when he wrote the same. The mark purporting to be the mark of the deceased was put to the codicil by Green and attached by him to the will, which he delivered to Alice Arrowsmith, widow of the testator.

Dorothy Green of Whittingham, aged 23 and daughter of John Green, said the will shown to her was the same one that was signed, sealed and published in her presence, the same will the testator marked and sealed. The testator she considered was of perfect mind and memory at the time, but she did not remember hearing the will read over to the testator.

Replying to the questions put by the executors Sittgreave and Duckworth, Dorothy stated that she heard her father declare that the codicil was written by him the morning after Richard Arrowsmith died and was written in her father's house at Whittingham. She also added that there was no one with him when he wrote the same. She believed that her father wrote the codicil in accordance with directions he had received during the testator's lifetime. Certainly her father delivered this to Alice Arrowsmith the day following Arrowsmith's death. The mark placed on the codicil as the mark of Richard Arrowsmith was put there by John Green her father.[17] The codicil was rejected and Green excommunicated.

A lengthy dispute arose over the nuncupative will of James

Morgan, spurrier of Clevely, who was also a shoemaker, between William Richmond, the residual legatee, and John Walton of Lancaster, uncle of James Morgan, who died 20 November 1728. Edward Fox of Cleveley, a turner aged 30, said that James Morgan lodged at his house in Cleveley at the time of his death and had also worked in a shop within the house since the previous March. On Monday 28 October, he went to see the deceased, who was then ill in bed at Fox's house, being very much indisposed. William Richmond of Cleveley, the deceased's master, went with him and no other persons.

Richmond asked the deceased if he would have any relatives sent for or if he would dispose of everything he had to them. Morgan replied: 'No, I am in the same mind. You shall bury me and give to the poor and take the rest yourself.' The document annexed to the allegation was the will of James Morgan of Cleveley, shoemaker, witnessed by John Townson and James Holmes, and the witness was satisfied that it was the will of the deceased. The will was dated 2 November 1725; the deceased lived until the Wednesday night following.

Fox said that the deceased had a very close relationship with William Richmond, for both had worked together in the same shop in Cockerham about four or five years ago, then Morgan came to Cleveley to be a servant with William Richmond, which was in March last, and so continued in his service until his death.

Morgan had a great respect for William Richmond, more than any other person, but Fox had never heard when Morgan was healthy that he would leave what he had to William Richmond. The only relative Morgan had in England was John Walton of Lancaster, who was uncle to the deceased, as he had heard and believed.

William Richmond, according to the deceased's will, had buried him decently and 'did give and distribute a dole to the Poor vizt 2^d a piece to Some and 1^d and bread and cheese to others and there were a great many poor that resorted to the Funeral and received the Dole accordingly'.

In response to the questions put to him on the part of John Walton, Fox said that Morgan lodged with him from the previous March until his death. He believed that he did not die possessed of any goods except 25 guineas and 9s. His apparel and work tools would not amount to 30s.; his apparel being but very cheap, was worth about 10s. The true value of the tools he did not understand, but supposed they were not of any great value. He was present when the deceased declared his mind, but he did not think that he would have done so if William Richmond had not asked him about sending for some of his friends on the disposing of his effects. At that point he declared his will very freely and was not in the least embarrassed when declaring his mind. He also heard William Richmond declare that Morgan had given him the 25 guineas, saying as he did so, 'Here, take this drosse, Lord what a work I have had in getting this far in 20 years' – a fitting comment on the hard life of a shoemaker which brought so little return. He continued his evidence by stating that he had heard John Walton say that Morgan had a father living in Ireland, but he could not recall that he heard the deceased ever mention him or that he planned any favours to him, neither had he heard Richmond at any time solicit Morgan to make his will in Richmond's favour.

Fox said that Morgan had never asked him to act as a witness or say that what he declared should be taken for his will. Neither had he heard Morgan give any reason why he refused to make a bequest to his father or his sister, or in fact to any other relative. However, he had heard Morgan say that 'his father had gott 5^{li} of him when in Ireland and that hee would have had it again but that he could not gett it, whereupon he was displeased with his father'.

William Richmond lodged with Fox, and Morgan also resided there at the time of his death, but not in the same room. He had never heard that Morgan was ever asked if he wished John Walton to be sent for, because he was Morgan's nearest relative he now had in England. It appeared to Fox that Morgan, all the time he was with Richmond, never wanted for anything, for Richmond attended the deceased during the time of his sickness and provided for him whatever he desired.

John Richardson, the blacksmith of Cleveley, when called said that Morgan was a very close friend of William Richmond and that they worked as shoemakers with Thomas Barker at Cockerham five or six years ago, until last March when Morgan came to live in Cleveley.

Morgan, it appears, was one of the group, which included John Richardson and William Richmond, who met regularly at the Old Hollins Inn in Garstang. Meeting one evening a short

time before the previous Michaelmas, certain in the company
asked Morgan to show them his guineas: 'a wager being made
before how many Guineas would reach over the Table, in order
to decide which wager, the deceased was prevailed upon to
produce his Guineas which were Saw'd [*sic*] up in a Cloth &
where . . . there were 25 Guineas.' When the wager had been
settled, Richardson asked Morgan who was to have these after
he was dead, to which Morgan replied: 'My master shall have
them, every one.'

A week before Morgan's death, at All Saints last, Richardson
was present in Richmond's shop in Cleveley where Morgan was
working. During the course of the conversation, Richardson
understood that Morgan came from Ireland. His curiosity being
aroused, he asked Morgan if he had served his apprenticeship in
that country. Morgan replied that he served his apprenticeship
with John Walton of Lancaster, who was his uncle. Like so
many youngsters who were apprenticed to a craft with relatives,
Morgan was shockingly abused. He said that 'John Walton had
abused him to that Degree that he made him so decrepit and
lame as he was and spoke very angrily of John Walton'. So, in
accordance with Morgan's wishes, Richmond had buried him
decently and provided a dole for the poor.

John Richmond of Ellell, a shoemaker, confirmed that he knew
both James Morgan and William Richmond, for they had all
worked together with Thomas Barker in Cockerham some
four years ago. He was convinced that Morgan and William
Richmond were very close friends. The previous March Morgan
had come to work for William Richmond as a journeyman
shoemaker until his death.

In the previous August John Richmond was at the alehouse of Timothy Winder in the company of Morgan and
Richmond when Morgan brought out a stocking and placed
it on the table.

He then took out of his stocking several Guineas which
were wrapped up in a peice of Leather and there were
24 and a half and the witness remembered that Morgan
had said William Richmond had been a kind master to
him and that he should have his Guineas should he dye
in Richmond's service.

He too had heard Morgan say how he was so abused by John

Walton, his uncle, that the beatings were the cause of his lameness. He also confirmed that he had known the parties in the cause for twenty years and that they were all reliable witnesses. In the end the court found in favour of William Richmond and granted probate of the will.[18]

In 1729 the will of George Kilner, mariner, late of Foulyate in Cartmel, was contested by his nephews, Thomas Kilner and Miles Walker, against William Kilner alias Robinson of Cartlane. John Carter of Cartlane said that George Kilner was his neighbour and when he heard that he was indisposed he went to visit him. Whilst he was with the testator he was requested to draw his will, which he consented to do. So he drew the will under the direction of George Kilner, and this was some seven years ago. At the time, James Seatle and William Robinson, as well as Thomas Leather, were present when the will was drawn and they subscribed their names to the paper and dated it 30 April 1722.

Sometime during May 1722 the will was proved before Mr Brooksbank, surrogate for the rural dean of Furness. George Kilner's mother undertook to act as executrix until she died. It is clear that there were some shipping interests in which Kilner and Walker were involved but at the time they made no objection to the will so far as the shipping interest was involved to get the will rejected. Although William Robinson alias Kilner was one of the residuary legatees, he was a single man and in no way related to either of the subscribing witnesses for 'upwards of two if not three years'.

Thomas Seatle of Cartlane, yeoman, said that when he heard of George Kilner's illness, and being his nearest neighbour, he went to visit him at Foulyate where the deceased lived. Kilner asked John Carter, who was also a visitor, to draw his will, which Carter obligingly did. The draft was then read over to the testator, who marked and sealed it, the witnesses subscribing their names. In his opinion the testator was of perfect mind and memory when he made his will and appointed his mother Esther Kilner as his executrix.

According to Seatle, the will was proved seven years before by the vicar of Cartmel, who was acting as surrogate for the rural dean, and he never heard that any objections were raised by either of the plaintiffs in this cause till after the death of Esther Kilner, nor did anyone attempt to annul the will.

During his cross-examination, John Carter said that he was never sent for to act as a witness to the will, but was visiting as a friend and neighbour when the will was drawn up. He witnessed the will of his own free will and not under pressure from any one. Thomas Smith also confirmed that he would never swear that George Kilner was insensible at the time he made his will, neither had he received or been promised any reward for acting as a witness by William Robinson. He had no knowledge that John Carter had said that he was prepared to spend £300 or any other sum of money on the defence of this suit or that he would defray the charges. It appeared that there was a report in the parish that William Robinson was courting Carter's daughter in order that he would be able to marry her and inherit before the testator died.

Ann Barrow of Foulyate in Cartmel, aged 25, said that some seven years previously, she went to visit George Kilner since she had heard that he was very ill, and that was in April. After some short conversation with him concerning his welfare, she saw Thomas Chapman of Grange was writing in the room where the deceased then lay.

> Whereupon, she was requested to withdraw, after some short time, and was informed by the testator's mother that George was making his will. Whereupon she went into the next neighbour's House and returned to see him at which time Thomas Chapman and the other persons were gone.

She noted how sensible the testator was by his conversation with herself and others who were present. The next day she heard that John Carter of Cartlane had drawn the will, and the following night she 'waked' with the deceased before he died. At the time the deceased was in great pain but sensible and she was put under no pressure to leave, although he only lived another night. The upshot was that both Kilner and Walker wanted the will made by Chapman overturned as irregular, an argument that was accepted by the court.[19]

The will of Thomas Robinson of Liverpool, mariner, dated 10 January 1661, reveals the jealousy that could arise concerning bequests that involved ships and shipping. Hannah Owen, sister-in-law of the testator, claimed to be the principal legatee and that she should have the right to act as administrator in the place of his sister, Elizabeth Sancelott, and her husband. The will was declared and committed to writing. On 20 September 1661, Thomas Robinson expressed his mind and will, 'being sick of the sickness from which he died'.

> It was his will and mind that hee did give, dispose and bequeath to his sister in law Hannah Owen of Liverpool, spinster, his half share of the shipp or vessel called the Anne. She the said Hannah paying to her father John Owen the sum of five pounds which the testator owed him and likewise his Funeral expenses though it should amount to tenn Pounds. Also whatever might Accrue or be due to him the said Robinson out of his brother Henry Robinson's estate, he desired it to be divided between his Mother, Anne Owen, his sister Elizabeth Sancelott and his kinsman John Sancelott.

He had declared his will only two days before he died.[20]

It was the custom for a ship to be owned by a number of shareholders, who had contributed to its construction to enable them to have a share in the profits, since maritime trade was expanding rapidly and there were good profits to be made.[21] The court found for Robinson's closest relative as administrator, who was his sister and not his sister-in-law, on the grounds that she was no blood relation.

The relatives of John Wartopp of Dillaker, husbandman, who died in 1689, were annoyed when they found that they were not involved in the making of the will. The testator had appointed Agnes Atkinson, the wife of Edmund Atkinson, as his executor. The will was contested by John Nanson, Isabel Whitehead and Thomas Nanson, who said that he was Wartopp's neighbour and that on 4 July 1688 he called upon him and found him to be 'indisposed and out of health. He tabled with Edmund Atkinson, the husband of Agnes to whom he expressed a desire to draw his will for he knew not how soon God might call him out of this World'. Wartopp enquired if Joseph Airey, a neighbour, was at home but he was informed that he had 'gone abroad', in other words out of the district. So Atkinson sent for his son Richard to draw the will. Richard said that when he arrived he told the deceased that he was unwilling to draw the will because he was not accustomed to handling that type of business. However, he was persuaded to draw the will. Reading it over to the testator two or three times, he asked the testator if that was his will, and he agreed that it was. It was then signed, sealed, witnessed and published, which Atkinson confirmed to be correct. However, John Nanson and Isabel Whitehead, being close relatives, considered that they ought to have been consulted and involved in the matter. Probate was nevertheless granted to the executor.[22]

Instances do occur where the opponents to a will are no close relatives of the deceased. When George Livesey of Teal in Kirkham parish died in 1727, John and Adam Livesey, along with Jane Piper, contested the will against Catherine Livesey, his widow. Catherine Livesey said that, after George died, John Livesey, his father, was still in good health and living in Longridge. John Livesey was personally present at the funeral when George's brothers, John and Adam Livesey, as well as their sister Jane, conversed with their father. Catherine stated that Thomas, Adam and Henry Livesey, as well as Jane Piper, were none of them blood relations of George Livesey, who died intestate. Since she had married George Livesey, and Thomas, Adam and Jane were by her first husband, they had no right, nor were they entitled, to any part or share in the estate of the deceased, which by right belonged to Catherine, his widow, and John, his father. She also added that the parties opponent had neither right nor lawful interest to exhibit in court the inventory of the deceased's estate or to the administration. The parties opponent said that the inventory, which showed the value of live goods to be £27.15s. 0d., concealed the real number and value of the deceased's effects. Catherine declared and explained the full details before the court and she was granted the right to administer the estate.[23]

Failure to fulfil all legal requirements in connection with a will meant that the will could be declared null and void. The will of John Hodgson of Distington, who died in 1725, is a good example. Nathaniel Dickenson, a witness on the part of Abraham Hodgson, said that, when John Hodgson gave his instructions as to the disposal of his effects, he said that his son John should inherit the house and lands and enjoy them during his life.

Now Abraham Hodgson and his mother Ann Hodgson had other ideas, for they contrived with the cooperation of John Fearon to establish a pretended will in order to defraud John of his inheritance, hoping to obtain the lot for themselves. They also decide that Ann should renounce her title to execute the will and turn witness to the benefit of them both.

Their next step was to approach John Hodgson and offer him £5 to release Abraham from accounting for the goods he bought, worth £11, at the sale of his father's effects, and so allow Ann to witness to the pretended will. Their scheme was well planned but had one fatal flaw: Dickenson had omitted to record John's inheritance in the will. The court rejected the pretended will, declaring it to be null and void and it was to be treated as an intestate estate.[24]

Those who moved from one diocese to another could create a problem. When John Wood of Dalton died in 1729 he left a son, William, who was a 'doctor of medicine', Bridget Wood, his widow, and his daughter, Elizabeth, who had married Thomas Gibson, a merchant. John Wood died intestate and Bridget applied for letters of administration. In doing so she had forgotten her daughter, Elizabeth, who, extremely annoyed by the situation, challenged the right of Bridget to be the sole executor on the grounds that she was John's lawful daughter and so she was entitled to claim an equal degree of relationship to John Wood and to a share of his estate.

It then appeared that Thomas Gibson, John Wood's son-in-law, and John Wood were partners as merchants and Gibson claimed that he had had to lay out considerable sums of money on account of John Wood, so he was the principal creditor. In the meantime, William had left Dalton and moved to another practice outside the province of York and was therefore outside the jurisdiction of the consistory court. It was admitted that William Wood had already received £1,000 from his father as an advance on his 'child's part' out of his father's estate. It was decreed that Elizabeth, as the daughter of John Wood, was entitled to a share upon a distribution to be made according to the Statute in that case made and provided.[25]

It was stated in court that John Remington had died without issue in 1700 and his brother Thomas had predeceased him two years previously. Their sister Jane also died without issue in 1705 and was intestate, and their sister Elizabeth followed her to the grave in 1710, again without issue and intestate. In each case Robert Remington had been notified of the deaths of his brothers and sisters as soon as they had happened. Several times the apparitor had cited him to appear in court and prove the wills of the deceased relatives or take out letters of administration. All these things Robert Remington stubbornly refused to do, so he was considered to be in contempt of the law as well as of the authority and jurisdiction of the court because he,

> of his own accord and temerity without any lawfull author-
> ity possessed himself of all the several shares, proportions
> & personal estates of the said parties deceased which did
> belong to them at the time of their deaths.
> The Law states that those who of their own will take
> the goods and chattels of any deceased are, ipso facto
> excommunicated and should be denounced.

It was precisely on these grounds that letters of administration for the estates of John, Thomas and Elizabeth Remington were granted to their brother Richard, who had sworn his oath and entered bond for the due administration of the estates of these intestate persons according to law. Since Robert Remington had for so long rejected the same, it was agreed that he be dismissed with costs and the allegation stated should be entered into court; Robert Remington was sentenced with full costs and also excommunicated.[26]

Tithes and other dues that were payable to an incumbent in a parish were recoverable at law on his death, when his widow could lay claim to receive payment of these. In 1679 there was a cause of this type in Ashes in Askrigg chapel when James Nelson denied that he should pay any dues whatsoever. Maria Janson, widow of Tristram Janson, late curate, said that,

> there is a laudable custom observed within the parish
> that, all and singular proprietors, occupiers or owners
> of dwelling houses should pay annually at Easter certain
> alms, fourpence in legal money of England to the minister
> or curate celebrating divine service in the same chapel.

Now Tristram Janson had been curate of Askrigg chapel between 1675 and 1679. Meanwhile, John Wilson occupied a dwelling house in Askrigg in 1677, 1678 and 1679, and so owed dues of 4d. to Tristram Janson, who died in 1679. James Nelson now occupied Wilson's house and he too should have paid his dues of 4d. to Janson. Maria Janson sought to have the debt paid by order of the court. The money was recovered from Wilson but Nelson was sentenced to pay full costs.[27]

A testator who was identified by an alias could give rise to a great deal of disagreement between relatives. Such was the cause concerning the will of William Morgan alias James of Gloucester. The suit was commenced by Margaret James, who claimed to be the natural daughter of Jeremiah James of Farmington, who claimed to be the natural brother of William Morgan deceased, and who was being challenged by William Ridley alias Gregory, who claimed blood relationship, as to which of the two ought to be the legal administrator of the deceased's goods.

It was alleged that William Morgan alias James, whose goods were in contest for rightful administration, was the natural son of one Morgan who had married Agnes, daughter of Henry James of Greet in the parish of Winchcombe,

> on whose body Morgan the father did after wedlock begett William Morgan deceased. Also Morgan the father was never surnamed James but was a Morgan only. His son William Morgan deceased was not a James by his surname but a Morgan only. Because his father died before William was born or shortly after and his mother also died when he was young, so his uncle on his mother's side brought him up for which reason he was called William Morgan alias James, and not otherwise so named.

Now Charles James (the uncle of William Morgan and brother of Agnes James), who was acting as guardian of young William, bound him apprentice by the name of William Morgan and not by the name of William Morgan alias James. Later he became apprenticed to 'one Richard Creswell of Didsbrooke a slatter after to John Glasyer of Wynchcombe and then afterwards to one Wager of Gloucester'.

When Morgan had completed his apprenticeships and become of full age he was made a freeman of the city of Gloucester and by the name of William Morgan and not James. He then made an approach to the Dean and Chapter of Gloucester for a lease of three tenements, with their appurtenances, and a garden in the parish of St Mary le Soad for forty years in the name of Morgan and not James.

William Ridley, the defendant in this cause, had married

Agnes James, the daughter of Charles James, who was the uncle of William James on his mother's side. However, neither Charles James nor Henry Morgan were of any blood relationship to Margaret James the plaintiff or to John James his father. Also, neither Margaret nor John were ever called Morgan for their surname, but only James, as various witnesses deposed.

The evidence given by Lawrence Sydall and Walter Whitney of Farmington was said to be vacillating in every part of it. It was claimed that William Ridley alias Gregory was a poor man, and therefore extremely unreliable, who for mere 'profit and rewards will swear and depose anything be it never so untrue'. Faced by so damning a statement, the decree went in favour of Margaret James.[28]

Another person who was involved in an illegal manner concerning an estate was James Wilkinson. The will of George Wilkinson, a butcher from Tewkesbury, was defended by William Hammond, his son-in-law, innkeeper of Tewkesbury, and Elizabeth, his wife, against James Wilkinson of Twels, a cordwainer by trade. The will exhibited in court by James Wilkinson was dated 28 November 1737, and was approved by the judge. Letters of administration were granted to James Wilkinson, who had 'intermeddled and acted falsely in disposing of the goods, rights & Credits' of George Wilkinson. The testator left to Elizabeth Hammond the sum of £10 to be paid to her 'four months after my death'. George Wilkinson left sufficient money to pay all his debts and expenses. When James Wilkinson was asked to pay the legacy he openly refused, hence the request to the court that he be sentenced to pay the costs of the cause.[29]

An excellent example of a dispute between two close relatives is to be found in the cause of Sarah Vyner against Robert Vyner junior of Stroud. Although the cause was heard in 1691, the background to it was laid in 1657. Daniel Hatton, a broadcloth weaver of Stroud, where he was born and lived all his life, said that in 1657 he saw the late Robert Vyner the elder sign the lease of a 'cottage or tenement' near Stroud which was made between Robert Vyner for the one part and Mary, his wife, with Elizabeth of the other part who were involved in the lease of the cottage. Hatton had also seen several 'very antient deeds & conveyances' to which Robert Vyner deceased had written his name and he had also seen Robert Vyner junior sign his name to several writings. He was very well acquainted with Vyner, but for five or maybe six years before he died he had no contact with him because Hatton had left Stroud to live elsewhere and came to Stroud only to pay his rent. He remembered hearing Robert Vyner say that he would give his property at Stroud to Sarah and Margaret Vyner, his daughters.

Another broadcloth weaver, Anthony Paul, said he had lived in Stroud for sixty years and had openly heard Robert Vyner say that he would make provision for his daughters. In 1654, the witness signed the lease of a cottage with Robert Vyner in Stroud. He paid the interest to Sarah Vyner as a rent charge of 8s. per annum, but he denied having been paid to come to court. Replying to questions put to him, Paul said that seven years before Vyner died he discussed with him very reasonably and his mind was clear. He was 80 years of age when he died but had no idea whether or not he was able to write.

Mary Castle of Ramswick, who had lived for thirty years in Gloucester, said that when Robert Vyner was sick she went to visit him in Painswick, intending also to speak with Robert Vyner junior, but he was absent from home. She was invited by Sarah Vyner to go upstairs to see her father, who was pleased to see her and praised the 'dutifullness of his daughter'. It was made clear to her that his two sons were very different, for Robert Vyner said that they 'were undutifull and would not visit him in his sickness. He would make them repent that they had not come on their bare feet to see him'. He also informed her that he had lands, corn and houses in Stroud and also corn, grain and cattle at Painswick, for he was a prosperous yeoman.

It soon became clear from the evidence that Robert Vyner junior would attempt to overthrow his father's will. Maria Hillman of Painswick and wife of Richard Hillman said she was born at Llanbadock in Radnor and was now 50 years old. Some five days before Robert Vyner senior died, she was in the presence of Sarah Vyner when she heard her say that her brother Robert would endeavour to make void his father's will. Maria Hillman replied that she hoped it would not come to that because he had left all that he possessed by deed and will to his daughters, Sarah and Margaret Vyner, and would take care 'to see they were not cheated of what he had left her sister Margaret. The very last words he spoke were, "my daughter Sarah pray fervently for me" and then he expired'.

Then some intimate character descriptions were provided for the witnesses of Robert Vyner junior. Mary Castle affirmed that both Edward Baker and John Escourt were well known to her but they were persons of no credit and their evidence would be suspect. On the other hand, both Edmund Newark and Richard Wiltsheir, as well as Mary Wiltsheir, were persons of good reputation and standing in the community and would not under any circumstances be found guilty of perjury.

Further information was added by William Bradley, farmer of Cranham, who had lived for thirty-five years in that parish, having been born at Syde, and who was now 70 years old. He was very well informed about John Escourt and Elizabeth Bissell, witnesses on the part of Robert Vyner, stating that Escourt was a man who 'promotes strife and contention among his neighbours who was presented a year ago at Brimpsfield court for a common Barrator & disturber of his neighbours'. He added that 'Elizabeth Bissell has had a bastard and she is a person of noe credit or reputation'.

Then Bradley provided a piece of damning evidence against John Escourt of forging an entry in the parish register and he also provided some interesting information. Some twelve years previously he had lent the parish registers to John Escourt, who refused to return them until some three months ago, when he discovered that Escourt had 'with his own hand feisted [entered] into the said book that Sarah daughter of Robert Newark was christened, but upon what day or year he cannot now remember'. He had no opinion of John Escourt's wife, Sarah Newark, for she 'was a person of noe credit and made it her business to carry lyes and stories from one neighbour to another ... who has been presented at Brimpsfield court for a scold'. He considered that William Newark was a very charitable man, of complete honesty and integrity. At one time he was a regular attender at Painswick church but 'for the past two or three years he has flighted the Church ... and believes this to be occasioned by his deafness'.

Bradley was very suspicious about Elizabeth Sadler, who was found to be associating with Elizabeth Whitacres, who 'four or five years since killed her husband'. In fact, Bradley reported Elizabeth Sadler and others for being in the company of Elizabeth Whitacres at the time she killed her husband. In an attempt to take revenge on Bradley she brought an action 'at Law against Bradley for presenting her' but she lost her case and served a period of imprisonment, but since that time 'she has lived soberly, quietly and peaceably among her neighbours'.

John Sadler of Cranham, yeoman, who had been born at Watton Barrett in Wiltshire and who was now 60 years of age, had nothing of credit to say about Escourt and his wife Sarah. John Escourt was nothing more than a common barrator and his wife Sarah had been before the Brimpsfield court as a scold. He claimed that Sarah was the natural daughter of Elizabeth Bissell, who was 'a person of noe credit' and, according to repute, never married. Meanwhile John Escourt, while he had the parish registers in his possession, had 'entered into the book that Sarah daughter of Robert Newark was christened', but no other details were given.

Elizabeth the wife of John Sadler, who had been accused of consorting with the murderess Elizabeth Whitacres, had no opinion of the standing of the Escourts in Cranham society. She had been born at Lydiatt Tregoze in Wiltshire and had lived in Cranham for twenty years, being now 30. She affirmed that 'Sarah Escourt was with child when they were married and she is the daughter of Elizabeth Bissell who never married'. Likewise she had no time for Edward Baker the parish busybody, who 'had much better meddle more with his own business & less with that of his neighbours'.

After weighing all the evidence, the court found in favour of Sarah Vyner; her brother Robert lost his attempt to overthrow the will and was sentenced to pay the full costs.[30]

Occasionally one receives insight into other aspects of community life as revealed in a contested will. In 1665, Richard White owned a distillery in Chipping Sodbury. Richard had little time to make his will, so he dictated it to witnesses. He died before his mother. To Susan White, his wife, he left that part of his house in Chipping Sodbury which his mother now inhabited. His mother, for whom he had to make provision, was to receive that part of the house which comprised 'the Little Hall leading into the Forestreet Chamber'. He then proceeded to divide the rest of his effects.

The Warehouse and half the Cellar, the Backside during the whole term of her life with all the outhousing thereto belonging. And he did give unto his wife the Coffer which was in his Mother's Chamber standing by the Bedds head with all the Linnen that was in the said Coffer. And he also gave to his wife halfe his Stills and his Furnace and other Implements belonging to the making of Strong Waters. And he gave to his wife all the goods Chattels and Household Stuffe and he did appoint Richard Hick and his wife's daughter to be his executors.[31]

Thus, by dividing his business interests between his wife and his daughter, he ensured that his widow would have an income on which she could live.

There is, of course, tragic evidence of alienation in families often motivated by greed. One such cause involved John Piper against his widowed mother.

In 1701, a letter from John Birkett to Josias Lambert, the Registrar at Kendal, asked Lambert to speak to the proctor, who was acting for John Piper. In his letter he points out that 'No man would have the face to do so wickedly for he entered into all the Goods of his father and left his Mother to pay a debt of thirty three pounds'. Unable to clear the debt, she was arrested and thrown into prison. Fortunately for her, she had some land of her own, which she was able to realize and so obtain her freedom. John Piper, it was revealed, had not only taken sixty head of cattle but also the butcher's shop and the horses, one of which was valued at £3 but Piper sold it for £5 to Mr Ewood. There was also a mare valued at 20s. but sold for £5 and, as Birkett suggested to Lambert, 'so you may guess the rest'. Josias Lambert proposed that the court should appoint someone to act as administrator so that Mrs Piper's debts and her late husband's legacies could be paid. The court took this advice and the poor woman was cleared.[32]

15

CONCLUSION

The examination of some 450 contested wills brought before the
consistory court has revealed the full extent of human weakness.
One feature stands out most clearly and that is that the seven
deadly sins appear to be very much alive and in an excellent state
of health. Two of these sins are emphasized in this study: those
of avarice and envy. In nearly every case the cupidity of both
plaintiffs and defendants is revealed by the manner in which
they set out to obtain as large a share of the estate, the goods
and the chattels as they can manage to lay their hands upon.

One common feature that appears to be prominent in
most contested wills is the 'expectancy of inheriting'. These
expectancies amount to little more than promises which could
be broken, if the testator so desired. This point is well illustrated
in the cause of Barrow v Benn at Whitehaven. Barrow, like many
others before and since, assumed that, when Benn said that he
could have his pew in Whitehaven church and his silver punch
bowl, he literally meant what he said. Many people when in
a state of inebriation make promises to those who see them
safely home from the alehouse; and Benn really believed them.
He founded his expectations upon the promises being fulfilled.
When Barrow discovered that the contrary had happened and a
relative had received the two items, he was so overwhelmed with
envy that he instigated a suit in the consistory court, convinced
that he could get the will overturned. To his discomfort, the
poor man lost and was faced with the prospect of paying the
legal costs.

In fact, throughout this study the evidence produced shows
that causes of this type serve only to bring into full view
the worst side of human relationships. Sons-in-law would

frequently bring influence to bear upon their wives to stake a claim to more of their deceased father's estate than they were entitled to, making such remarks as 'if there is any money in this estate I am having it'. Occasionally a father tries to keep a check on his wayward offspring, commenting, 'If I gave them all I had they would only spend it'.

So, overcome by their desires to acquire as much of the estate as possible, the plaintiffs contrived a number of often devious ways to achieve their ends.

Accusations flew around that the deceased had been subject to undue influence at a critical time during his or her last illness. The argument was also presented that the will was written after the testator died, sometimes a gap of four days occurring between the testator's death and the writing of the will. There were causes, such as the one from Arksey, where two wills were produced, one either out of date or else forged. There were also cases where the inventories were said to be false or forged, or the goods and chattels were grossly undervalued – but no one seems to claim that the goods were overvalued or even that there had been overt misappropriation of goods. The problem of debt was a regular theme in many causes. Very few died without money owing to them or creditors who were anxious to have their loans or accounts settled. In the pre-industrial society, such as the one covered by this study, additional finance was raised by lending to or borrowing from one's friends or relatives.

In the uncertain world of the seventeenth and eighteenth centuries, accidents and disease could quite easily terminate life abruptly, so that some died insolvent, leaving creditors bemoaning their losses and relatives worried about the soundness or otherwise of the debts due to the testator. There were other allegations brought, that the deceased was either 'crazed in his mind', or 'sick of a dumb palsy' or in no condition to make a will, and by these means relatives sought to achieve their aims.

The legal profession was not so well organized or disciplined as regards local solicitors as it is today, nor had the standards of practice been brought under the strict control that exists today. Schoolmasters, parish clerks, clergy, even laymen, were all considered to be capable of drawing up a will. When Butterworth, the curate of Penwortham, drew up a will he revealed his ignorance when he administered the estate, albeit a small one, without taking out letters of administration; he found himself in court.

William Wood, solicitor, of Halifax and Richard Collinson of Warton drew up wills in an unscrupulous manner by working upon unsuspecting clients to give them full power to structure the will, which was usually made in favour of the solicitor, only to be detected by one means or another during probate. Widows of marriageable age rarely remained in that state long, but were quickly invited to enter into matrimony with a second or even a third husband if their prospects were good.

One feature that stands out in many of these contested wills is the increasing prosperity of the more enterprising yeomen, husbandmen, weavers, stonemasons and craftsmen in general. Society was on the way to becoming a consumer society and, as the Gloucestershire wills reveal, an increasingly mobile one. The upper ranks of society were doing very well on the whole and seeking an outlet for their surplus funds. Naturally, because of the closeness of late seventeenth- and early eighteenth-century society, the enterprising methods of the upper echelons of that society tended to extend down to the lower ranks, although they excluded the very poor.

It is clear that our ancestors tended to be fond of litigation. To us who live at the close of the twentieth century, many of the causes concerning contested wills appear to involve too trivial a matter upon which to base a sound case that would conclude in the court one way or the other.

After nearly two thousand years of Christian teaching in this country, these contested wills reveal the virtual non-existence of 'living in love and charity with all men'; rather the reverse is in the evidence quoted in many of the cases. So the comments of Archbishop William Melton in 1329 on Christian attitudes may be an apt conclusion to this study: 'Christianity is but a thin veneer over a vast morass of barbarism.'

NOTES

1 INTRODUCTION

1 Rubric in the Order for the Visitation of the Sick, Book of Common Prayer, 1662.
2 Mortuary dues were eventually abolished in Chester Diocese in 1763, when the first voidance of Waverton Rectory took place after 1745 when abolition was decreed.
3 See the bills of taxed costs attached to many of the consistory court Cause Papers, Cheshire Record Office (CRO), EDC.5.

2 LAST WILLS AND TESTAMENTS

1 Henry Massie, *Ancient Law*, London, 1900, c. vi.
2 W. Pollock and F.W. Maitland, *History of English Law before the Time of Edward I*, Cambridge, 1898, vol. 2, 317.
3 CRO Cause Papers EDC.5, catalogued series.
4 G. Alexander, 'Custom of York', *Thoresby Society*, vol. 28, 1928.
5 Order for the Visitation of the Sick in the Book of Common Prayer, 1662.
6 Lancashire Record Office (LRO), Probate Causes, ARR/13/8, no. 80 Broughton.
7 Borthwick Institute of Historical Research (BIHR), Wills 1652, Sanderson.
8 13 Edward 1 c. 19, 31 Edward 3 c. 11.
9 32 Henry 8 c. 1; 34 & 35 Henry 8 c. 5.
10 22 & 23 Charles 2 c. 10; 1 James 2 c. 17.
11 Nuncupative wills are classified alongside the formal wills.
12 BIHR, Leeds wills 1648 (Whalley)
13 29 Charles 2 c. 3.
14 Alexander, op. cit.
15 See the depositions of the witnesses in the various causes to which reference is made.
16 LRO Rural Deans Court Books, ARR/37, 1664–1760.

3 PROBATE AND ADMINISTRATION

1 CRO, EDC.5 (1634), no. 25 Prestbury.
2 Leeds District Archives (LDA), Apparitors' Letter Books, RD/CA/1.
3 J. Addy (ed.), *The Diary of Henry Prescott*, Lancashire and Cheshire Record Society, no. 127, 1987.
4 M. Dansi, *Horae Decanicas Rurales*, London, 1855, vol. 2, 27.
5 H. Swinburner, *A Brief Treatise of Testaments and Wills*, London, 1890.
6 BIHR, Chancery Act Books, CH.AB.

4 IN SICKNESS AND IN HEALTH

1 E. Horsfall Turner (ed.), *The Diaries of Oliver Heywood*, Brighouse, 1897, *passim*.
2 M.F.M. Mulgrow (ed.), *The Parish Registers of St Mary, Castlegate, York, 1705–1837*, Yorkshire Parish Register Society, 1972, 217.
3 T.W. Hanson (ed.), *The Diary of Cornelius Ashworth of Waltroyd*, Transactions of the Halifax Antiquarian Society, 1916, 233–48.
4 J. Addy (ed.), *The Diary of Henry Prescott, vol. 1: 1704–1710*, Lancashire and Cheshire Record Society, no. 127, 1987, 286.
5 J. Addy (ed.), 'The Diary of Henry Prescott, vol. 2: 1711–1719', typescript, 227.
6 Addy, *Diary of Henry Prescott*, vol. 1, 9.
7 J. Archer, *Every Man his Own Doctor*, London, 1673.
8 W, Matthews (ed.), *The Diary of Dudley Ryder*, London, 1959, 196.
9 Addy, *Diary of Henry Prescott*, vol. 1, 186.
10 LDA, Ripley Parish Papers, CD/PB/7.
11 P. Earle, *The Making of the English Middle Class*, London, 1989, 304.
12 York Corporation House Books, York City Archives.
13 L.A. Clarkson, *Death, Disease and Famine in Pre–Industrial England*, Dublin, 1975, 103–5.
14 Addy, *Diary of Henry Prescott*, vol. 1, 14, 178.
15 Lord Wharncliffe and W. Thomas (eds), *Letters and Works of Lady Mary Wortley Montagu*, London, 1887, vol. 2, 186.
16 J. Addy, *Sin and Society*, London, 1989, 87.
17 ibid., 146.
18 ibid., 139.

5 DEATH AND BURIAL

1 T.E. Page (ed.), *Horace, Odes*, book 1, Carmen iv, London, 1925.
2 Francis Bacon, 'Essay on Death', *Essays of Bacon*, no. ii, Oxford, 1930.
3 Book of Common Prayer, Psalm 90, v10.
4 J. McManners, *Death and the Enlightenment*, Oxford, 1981, 228.
5 ibid., 227.

6 J. Moor, *A Map of Man's Mortality*, London, 1617, 10–11.
7 J. Addy, *The Diary of Henry Prescott*, vol. 1: *1704–1710*, Lancashire and Cheshire Record Society, no. 127, 1987, 178.
8 ibid., 226.
9 ibid.
10 P. Earle, *The Making of the English Middle Class*, London, 1989, 302.
11 LRO, Probate Causes, ARR/13/8, no. 171 Claughton.
12 LRO, Lancashire Contested Wills, DR.Ch.25 (1662) Liverpool.
13 LRO, Probate Causes, ARR/13/8, no. 187 Lamplugh.
14 C. Gittings, *Death, Burial and the Individual in Early Modern England*, London, 1984, 66.
15 J. Donne, 'Devotions upon Emergent Occasions', *Oxford Book of English Verse*, Oxford, 1925, 169–72.
16 BIHR, Archdeacon of York's Court Book, V/Y (1676).
17 Addy, op. cit., 132.
18 W.E. Tate, *The Parish Chest*, Cambridge, 1969, 68. The author, during an archaeological survey, came upon a lead coffin in which was the woollen cloth with which the body had been wrapped, according to the Statute.
19 Alexander Pope, *Epistles to Several Persons*, Epistle: *To Lord Cobham* (1734).
20 The author when a very young man was involved in the duty of inviting friends to funerals.
21 Addy, op. cit., 227–8.
22 J. Addy, 'The Diary of Henry Prescott 1715', typescript.
23 CRO, EDC.5 (1701), no. 18 Bolton.
24 CRO, EDC.5 (1718), no. 13 Ormskirk.
25 CRO, Contested Wills (1672) Ashton.
26 CRO, EDC.5 (1684), no. 20 Chester.
27 Addy, Diary of Henry Prescott, vol. 1, 153.
28 ibid., 133–4.
29 R.V.H. Burne, *Chester Cathedral*, London, 1958, 172.
30 CRO, EDC.5 (1639), No. 41 Ribchester.
31 LDA, Commissary's Act Book, RD/A/6 f.53.
32 J.S. Purvis, *Tudor Parish Documents*, Cambridge, 1948, 160.
33 Gittings, op. cit., 105.
34 LDA, Richmond Glebe Terriers, RD/G/49 Sedbergh.
35 LDA, Churchwardens' Presentments, RD/CB/8/1, no. 112.
36 ibid., no. 79.
37 CRO, EDC.5 (1696), no. 14 Winwick.
38 BIHR, Archdeacon of York's Court Book, V/Y (1664) Wakefield.
39 LDA, Comperta Book 1679, RD/C/11 Askrigg.
40 BIHR, Archdeacon of York's Court Book, V/Y (1677), Luddennden.
41 LDA, Comperta Book 1679, RD/C/11 Gilling.
42 BIHR, Archdeacon's Court Book, V/ER (1680) Hull.
43 ibid., V/Y (1687) Wakefield.
44 Gittings, op. cit., 154.
45 Arval bread was a coarse cake composed of flour, water, yeast,

currants and caraway seeds. These cakes were 8 inches in diameter and were marked with a sign which in some way represented a cross.

46 Halifax Central Library, D262.
47 Addy, *Diary of Henry Prescott*, vol. 1, 250.
48 Gittings, op. cit., 158.
49 The author recalls the ample provision of food and drink at funerals until rationing and restrictions in 1940–50 caused the custom to lapse to some extent.
50 Gittings, op. cit., 157.
51 BIHR, Testamentary Cause Papers, CP/year.
52 ibid., CP/1717/6 Wakefield.
53 ibid., CP/1717/9 Felkirk.
54 ibid., CP/1733/6 Sheffield.
55 LRO, ARR/13/8, no. 61 Cockerham.
56 LRO, ARR/13/8, no. 224 Rawcliffe.
57 Gittings, op. cit., 157.
58 LRO, ARR/13/8, no. 209 Handley.
59 ibid., no. 226 Claughton.
60 CRO, EDC.5 (1725), nos 1–2.
61 LRO, ARR/13/8 no. 53 Newsham.
62 ibid., no. 209 Crooke.
63 ibid., no. 224 Cockerham.

6 THE SOCIAL SCENE

1 A. Everitt, 'The Market Town', in *The Agrarian History of England and Wales*, Cambridge, 1967, vol. iv.
2 J.D. Marshall, 'The Rise and Transformation of the Cumbrian Market Town 1660–1900', *Northern History*, vol. xix, 1981, 128–49.
3 J.A. Sharpe, *Early Modern England*, London, 1987, 78–85.
4 C.M.L. Bouch, *Prelates and People of the Lake Countries*, Kendal, 1948.
5 F. Walker, *Historical Geography of South West Lancashire before the Industrial Revolution*, Chetham Society, vol. ciii, 1939.
6 J. Parkinson, 'Tithe Causes and Agriculture in North Lancashire', B.Ed. dissertation, University of Leeds, 1975.
7 R. Unwin, 'Tradition and Transition; Market Towns of the Vale of York 1660–1830', *Northern History*, vol. xvii.
8 K.M. Bumstead, 'Bedale Wills and Inventories', *Yorkshire Archaeological Journal*, vol. 57, 1985, 163–77.
9 L. Stone, *Family Sex and Marriage in England 1500–1800*, Harmondsworth, Middx, 1977.
10 E. Shorter, *The Making of the Modern Family*, London, 1975, 197.
11 Sharpe, op. cit., 81.
12 J. Addy, *The Diary of Henry Prescott*, vol. 1: *1704–1710*, Lancashire and Cheshire Record Society no. 127, 1987, *passim*.
13 Sharpe, op. cit., 96.

14 ibid., 96.
15 W. Wright, *The Complete Tradesman*, Dublin, 1787, 3.
16 J.A. Sharpe, op. cit., 92–4.

7 FRAUDULENT EXECUTORS

1 LRO, ARR/13/8, no. 142 Garstang.
2 ibid., additional statement. Excommunication meant the severance of the persons sentenced from attendance at church. The greater excommunication meant complete severance from other Christians and prohibition of burial in the churchyard or marriage in church.
3 LRO, ARR/13/8, no. 323 Goosenargh.
4 ibid., no. 328 Goosenargh.
5 ibid., no. 286 Fulwood.
6 CRO, Contested Wills, CW1673 Chester.
7 LRO, ARR/13/8, no. 2 Ulverston.
8 ibid., no. 11 Whitehaven.
9 ibid., additional files.
10 LRO, ARR/13/8, no. 315 Border Rigg.
11 BIHR, CP/1727/6 Thorne.
12 BIHR, CP/1717/3 Fenwick.
13 BIHR, CP/1720/3 Halifax.
14 LRO, ARR/13/8, no. 152 Silverdale.

8 FALSE INVENTORIES

1 LRO, ARR/13/8, no. 29 Bispham.
2 ibid., no. 286 Fulwood.
3 ibid., nos 119 and 354 Ulverston.
4 LDA, RD/AC/1/2 Kirklington.
5 LRO, ARR/13/8, nos 69 and 210 Tatham.
6 ibid., no. 196 Beethom.
7 ibid., no. 57 Goosenargh.
8 LDA, RD/AC/1/2, no. 60 Coverham.
9 BIHR, CP/1717/9 Felkirk.

9 DEBTS AND DEBTORS

1 LRO, ARR/13/8, no. 224 Out Rawcliffe.
2 ibid., no. 154 Cockerham.
3 LRO, DR.Ch/CW Oldham.
4 Gloucester Diocesan Record Office (GDRO), B4/2, no. R9.
5 J. Addy, *The Diary of Henry Prescott*, vol. 1: *1704–1710*, Lancashire and Cheshire Record Society, no. 127, 1987. Prescott's Diary contains many references to financial problems of Henry and his colleagues.

10 LEGACIES AND BEQUESTS

1 LDA, RD/AC1/2, no. 32 Richmond.
2 LRO, ARR/13/8, no. 167 Woodplumpton.
3 ibid., no. 152 Lindale.
4 ibid., no. 97 Kirby Lonsdale.
5 LDA, RD/AC1/4, no. 31 Melsonby.
6 GDRO, B4/2, no. B6.
7 CRO, CW Chester (1666).
8 LRO, ARR/13/8, no. 57 St Bees.
9 LRO, ARR/13/8, no. 289 Bispham.

11 THE CHILD'S PORTION

1 LRO, ARR/13/8, no. 112 Hawkshead.
2 ibid., no. 70 Melling.
3 ibid., no. 153 St Bees.
4 ibid., no. 47 Bowland.
5 BIHR, CW CP/1710.

12 TUTORS AND GUARDIANS

1 LRO, ARR/13/8, no. 155 Whitehaven.
2 ibid., no. 278 Millom.
3 CRO, EDC.5 (1725), no. 2 Liverpool.
4 LDA, RD/AC1/1, no. 5 Bedale.
5 GDRO, B4/2, no. A4.

13 NON COMPOS MENTIS

1 BIHR, CP/1738/5 Grimsargh.
2 J.S. Purvis, *The Records of the Admiralty Court of York*, York, 1962, 16–18.
3 LRO, ARR/13/8, no. 265 Whitehaven.
4 GDRO, B4/2, no. H12 Cirencester.
5 GDRO, B4/2, no. 90 Stonehouse.

14 NUNCUPATIVE WILLS

1 CRO, CW Chester (1699) Little Budworth.
2 CRO, CW Chester (1666) Audlem.
3 LRO, ARR/13/8, no. 171 Claughton.
4 ibid., no. 161 Preston.
5 LRO, DR.Ch.25 (1635) Middleton.
6 ibid. (1726) Chadderton.
7 ibid. (1661) Westhoughton.
8 CRO, CW Chester (1661) Ince.

9 LRO, ARR/13/8, no. 350 Urswick.
10 LRO, DR.Ch.17 Walton le Dale.
11 LRO, DR.Ch.25 Oldham.
12 GDRO, B4/2, no. G3 Gloucester.
13 ibid., no. C35 Yamsworth.
14 CRO, CW Chester (1661) Stoak.
15 LDA, RD/AC1/2, no. 72 Romaldkirk.
16 LRO, ARR/13/8, no. 343 Eskdale.
17 ibid., no. 319 Cleveley in Preston.
18 ibid., no. 324 Cleveley.
19 ibid., no. 346 Cartmel.
20 LRO, DR.Ch.25 Liverpool.
21 J.S. Purvis, *The Records of the Admiralty Court of York*, York, 1962, *passim*.
22 LRO, ARR/13/8, no. 212 Dillaker.
23 ibid., no. 284 Kirkham.
24 ibid., no. 277 Distington.
25 ibid., no. 332 Dalton.
26 ibid., nos 102, 104 and 111 Melling.
27 LDA, RD/AC1/2, no. 43 Askrigg.
28 GDRO, B4/2, no. M4 Gloucester.
29 ibid., no. W142 Tewkesbury.
30 ibid., no. V7 Stroud.
31 ibid., no. W24 Chipping Sodbury.
32 LRO, ARR/13/8, no. 93 Brigham.

BIBLIOGRAPHY

ORIGINAL SOURCES

Borthwick Institute of Historical Research, York
Archdeacon of York's Court Book Y/V 1674, 1677, 1687
Archdeacon of East Riding Court Book V/ER 1680
Testamentary Causes CP/Testament 1700–1800
Chancery Court Act Books CH/AB Wills

Cheshire Record Office
Chester Contested Wills CW 1660–1720
Consistory Court Act Books EDC 102–4
Consistory Court Files EDC 5 1639, 1685, 1701, 1718

Lancashire Record Office
Visitation Court Books ARR 37 1664–1760
Richmond Contested Wills ARR 13/8 Nos 1–350
Lancashire Contested Wills DRCh, 25

Leeds District Archives
Richmond Apparitors' Letter Books RD/CA
Commissary's Act Book RD/A/6
Churchwardens' Presentments RD/CB/8
Richmond Glebe Terriers RD/G
Richmond Contested Wills RD/AC/1–2
Richmond Parish Papers CD/PB/7

Gloucestershire Record Office
Gloucestershire Contested Wills B4/2

PUBLISHED SOURCES

Addy, J., *Sin and Society*, London, 1989.
Addy, J., (ed.), *The Diary of Henry Prescott*, Lancashire Record Society, vol. 127.

Alexander, G., 'Custom of York', *Thoresby Society*, 1928, vol. 28.

Archer, J., *Every Man his own Doctor*, London, 1673.

Bacon, Francis, *Essays of Bacon*, Oxford, 1930.

Bouch, C.M.L., *Prelates and People of the Lake Counties*, Kendal, 1948.

Bumstead, K.M., 'Bedale Wills and Inventories', *Yorkshire Archaeological Journal*, vol. 57, 1985.

Burn, R.V.H., *Chester Cathedral*, London, 1958.

Clarkson, L.A., *Death, Disease and Famine in Pre-Industrial England*, Dublin, 1975.

Dansi, M., *Horae Decanicae Rurales*, London, 1855, vol. 2, p. 27.

Donne, J., *Devotion upon Emergent Occasions*, Oxford, 1925.

Earle, P., *The Making of the English Middle Class*, London, 1989, p. 304.

Everitt, A., 'The market town', in *Agrarian History of England and Wales*, Cambridge, 1967, vol. iv.

Gittings, C., *Death, Burial and the Individual in Early Modern England*, London, 1984.

Hanson, T.W. (ed.), *The Diary of Cornelius Ashworth of Waltroyd*, Transactions of the Halifax Antiquarian Society, 1916, pp. 233–48.

Horsfall Turner, E. (ed.), *The Diaries of Oliver Heywood*, Brighouse, 1897, *passim*.

McManners, J., *Death and the Englightenment*, Oxford, 1981.

Marshall, J.D., 'The rise and transformation of the Cumbrian market town 1660–1900', *Northern History*, vol. xix, pp. 128–49.

Massie, H., *Ancient Law*, London, 1900, c.vi.

Matthews, W., (ed.), *The Diary of Dudley Ryder*, London, 1939, p. 196.

Moor, J., *A Map of Men's Mortality*, London, 1617.

Mulgrow, M.F.M. (ed.), *The Parish Registrars of St Mary, Castlegate, York 1705–1837*, Yorkshire Parish Register Society, 1972, p. 217.

Page, T.E. (ed.), *Horace Odes*, Book 1, 1925.

Parkinson, J., 'Tithe causes and agriculture in North Lancashire', B.Ed. dissertation for the University of Leeds, 1975.

Pollock, W. and Maitland, F.W., *History of English Law before the Time of Edward I*, Cambridge, 1898, vol. 2, p. 317.

Pope, Alexander, *Epistles to Several Persons*, London, 1734.

Purvis, J.S., *The Records of the Admiralty Court of York*, York, 1962.

Purvis, J.S., *Tudor Parish Documents*, Cambridge, 1948.

Sharpe, J.A., *Early Modern England*, London, 1987, pp. 78–85.

Shorter, E., *The Making of the Modern Family*, London, 1975, p. 197.

Stone, L., *Family, Sex and Marriage in England, 1500–1800*, Harmondsworth, 1977.

Swinburner, H., *A Brief Treatise of Testaments and Wills*, London, 1590.

Tate, W.E., *The Parish Chest*, Cambridge, 1969.

Unwin, R., 'Tradition and transition: market towns of the Vale of York 1660–1830, *Northern History*, vol. xvii.

Walker, F., *Historical Geography of South West Lancashire before the Industrial Revolution*, Chetham Society, vol. ciii, 1939.

Warncliffe, Lord and Thomas, W. (eds), *Letters and Works of Lady Mary Wortley Montagu*, London, 1887.

Wright, W., *The Compete Tradesman*, Dublin, 1787, p. 3.

INDEX

SUBJECTS

death: attitudes to 27, 28; fear of 26; hell 26, 27; violent 26
disease: small pox 19; venereal 24

funerals: burial 32; burials in gardens 38; costs 29; customs 36, 37; funeral cakes 41; funeral feasts 41–5; mourning periods 31; passing bell 29; preparation 30, 31; recusant burials 38; suicides' burial 38; undertakers 39; wakes 37, 38

Parliamentary Statutes: burial in woollen cloth, Act for 30; Distribution, Statute of 11; Frauds, Statute of 12; Uses, Statute of 11; Westminster 2; Wills, Act of, 1692 12; Wills, Statute of 11;

remedies; Bath waters 22; cannabis 23; Daffy's Elixir 20; herbal abortion 25; opium 23; Queen of Hungary's water 22; Saughton's Drops 23; Scarborough water 21; treacle water 23; White's Bitter Snake Root 21

wills: administrators 10, 14, 15;

Anglo-Saxon 8; custom of York 8, 12; drawing up of 9; executors 40, 44; inventories 47, 48; nuncupative 12; origin of 7; Personalty 7; probate 8, 15; Realty 7; Roman 7; testament 7; validity of 17

PERSONS

Abbott, Robert 36
Adey, John 109–11
Adey, Richard 109–11
Anyon, Alice 60
Anyon, Margaret 60, 61
apparitors 14
Appleyard, Samuel 71–2
Archer, John 21
Arkwright, John 81
Arkwright, Robert 44
Armistead, Jane 77, 80
Arrowsmith, Alice 130–1
Ashcroft, Edward 33
Ashmead, Mary 115
Ashton, John 84–5
Ashton, Thomas 38
Ashworth, Cornelius 19, 20
Atkinson, Agnes 137
Atkinson, George 114–15
Atkinson, Richard 137–8
Award, Thomas 59

Bacon, Francis 26
Baguley, John 85
Bailes, Christopher 129

PLACES